SECURED TRANSACTIONS

IN A NUTSHELL

FIFTH EDITION

By

RICHARD B. HAGEDORN

Rosalind VanWinkle Melton Professor of Law
College of Law, Willamette University

THOMSON

™

WEST

Mat #40533040

COPYRIGHT © 1976, 1981, 1988 WEST PUBLISHING CO.

© West, a Thomson business, 2000

© 2007 Thomson/West
      610 Opperman Drive
      St. Paul, MN 55123
      1–800–328–9352

Printed in the United States of America

ISBN: 978–0–314–17251–8

PREFACE

Perhaps a fitting student reaction to a course in Secured Transactions may be found in the following, which was supplied by an anonymous (presumed) student:

Yea thru the valley of the debts he has led us
    Tho I fear no evil
Because the debtor pays filing fees
    And file I must when the cause is almost just.

The purpose of this Nutshell is to discuss the law embodied in Article 9 of the Uniform Commercial Code on Secured Transactions, primarily as set forth in the 1999 version. Since the fourth edition of this Nutshell, all states have enacted the 1999 version. That version of Article 9 was actually approved in 1998 by the co-sponsoring bodies of the Uniform Commercial Code, the American Law Institute and the National Conference of Commissioners on Uniform State Laws. However, it is known as the 1999 version and shall be referred to as such throughout this Nutshell.

PREFACE

The discussion is comprehensive in scope, but necessarily limited in coverage of particular features of the law of secured transactions as embodied in Article 9 because this Nutshell is presented for use by students who seek a discussion of the basic elements of secured transactions law under the Code. The book should also be of aid to practicing attorneys who face problems in this area but lack experience in handling this particular area of law.

The author gratefully acknowledges the countless hours spent by Kathleen E. Marbut in preparing the text.

Richard B. Hagedorn

Salem, Oregon
May, 2007

Dedicated
To the Memory of

Professor Henry J. Bailey III

teacher, colleague and friend

OUTLINE

OUTLINE

CHAPTER 2.
THE SECURITY AGREEMENT

OUTLINE

CHAPTER 4. PERFECTION OF
SECURITY INTEREST

OUTLINE

OUTLINE

CHAPTER 5. PERFECTION OF SECURITY INTEREST BY FILING

OUTLINE

CHAPTER 6. CHOICE OF LAW AND PERFECTION IN MULTIPLE STATE TRANSACTIONS

OUTLINE

CHAPTER 8. BANKRUPTCY OR INSOLVENCY OF DEBTOR

OUTLINE

CHAPTER 9. DEFAULT AND
ENFORCEMENT OF SECURITY INTEREST

TABLE OF CITATIONS
to the
UNIFORM COMMERCIAL CODE

References are to Chapters (Ch.)
and Sections (§)

PRE-REVISION UCC ARTICLE 1

UCC CITATIONS

UCC CITATIONS

UCC CITATIONS

1999 UCC ARTICLE 9

UCC CITATIONS

UCC CITATIONS

UCC CITATIONS

UCC CITATIONS

UCC CITATIONS

UCC CITATIONS

UCC CITATIONS

UCC CITATIONS

SECURED TRANSACTIONS

IN A NUTSHELL

FIFTH EDITION

CHAPTER 1

INTRODUCTION

§ 1. Scope of Coverage; Uniform Commercial Code

a. History of UCC Article 9 – The 1962, Revised 1972 and 1999 Versions.

This Nutshell discusses *secured transactions* under Article 9 of the Uniform Commercial Code (the "Code" or the "UCC"). That Article primarily deals with secured transactions in most items of *personal property* (as distinguished from real property). With some individual state variations, Article 9 has been enacted in all the states, the District of Columbia, Guam, the North Mariana Islands, and the Virgin Islands. No part of the Code has been enacted in Puerto Rico.

The 1962 version of Article 9, once in force in most American jurisdictions, was superseded by the 1972 version in all jurisdictions.

The 1972 version of the Code was subsequently revised with technical changes to conform with later versions of other Articles of the Code. In 1994,

Article 9 also was revised to deal with security interests in investment securities under UCC Article 8 which also was revised in 1994.

This Nutshell primarily discusses the 1999 version of Article 9. In 1998, the Code sponsoring bodies (the American Law Institute and the National Conference of Commissioners on Uniform State Laws) approved an entirely new version of Article 9. That new version is referred to here as the 1999 Article 9, when it was submitted to the states for enactment. The 1999 Article 9 consists of a substantial reorganization of revised 1972 Article 9, a renumbering of most sections, and the inclusion of a number of new provisions. All jurisdictions that had enacted the revised 1972 version of Article 9 have replaced it by enacting the 1999 version. Limited discussion of the revised 1972 version is included in this Nutshell to provide historical perspective. The revised 1972 version of Article 9 is referred to here as the 1972 Article 9.

b. The Comments to the Code

Reference also is made at various places in this Nutshell to Official Comments to sections of the Uniform Commercial Code. For example, a reference to Comment 3 to 1999 § 9-103 is to the Official

Comment number 3 of the drafters which follows and discusses some aspect of § 9-103 of the 1999 version. Although the Comments to the various Code sections do not themselves have the force of statutory law, they are valuable aids in the interpretation of such Code sections and have been extensively utilized by courts in Code cases.

c. Other Writings

Secured Transactions under Article 9 of the Uniform Commercial Code is the subject of discussion in a large number of law review articles and published books. A Hornbook that deals extensively with Article 9 is White and Summers, Uniform Commercial Code, 5th ed., Student Edition, West Publishing Co., 2000. Article 9 (as well as other Articles of the Code) also is discussed in Stone, Uniform Commercial Code in a Nutshell, 6th ed., West Publishing Co., 2005. An exhaustive discussion of the background of secured transactions under the Code and under prior law is the early two-volume set, Gilmore, Security Interests in Personal Property, Little, Brown & Co., 1965, reprinted, Lawbook Exchange, 1999.

d. *Uniform Commercial Code Generally*

The Uniform Commercial Code deals with secured transactions, the subject matter of this Nutshell, in Article 9. Other aspects of commercial transactions are covered in other Articles of the Code. Thus, Article 2 deals with Sales, Article 2A with Leases, Article 3 with Negotiable Instruments, Article 4 with Bank Deposits and Collections, Article 4A with Funds Transfers, Article 5 with Letters of Credit, Article 7 with Documents of Title and Article 8 with Investment Securities. Article 6 deals with bulk transfers, but that Article was repealed in a number of states and revised in most remaining states.

Article 1 of the Code sets forth a number of General Provisions, including definitions of a number of terms and rules of construction, which affect all other Articles of the Code, including Article 9. Article 1 was recently revised. This Nutshell will refer to both pre-revision and revised Article 1. There are also provisions at the end of the UCC that deal with the effective date of the various Articles of the Code in the enacting jurisdiction, continue the validity of commercial transactions entered into before the effective date of the various Articles, and list statutes repealed by the Code.

While this Nutshell discusses secured transactions under Article 9, reference will be made where appropriate to provisions in other Articles of the Code, and particularly to various General Provisions and definitions in pre-revision and revised Article 1.

The Uniform Commercial Code was drafted during the period following World War II as a joint project of the American Law Institute and the National Conference of Commissioners on Uniform State Laws, referred to as the Code sponsors. The drafting represented the work of a large number of lawyers, judges, law professors and others. Later versions of the various Articles of the Code, including the 1999 version of Article 9, were drafted by other groups of lawyers, judges, law professors and others, again as a joint project of the American Law Institute and the National Conference of Commissioners on Uniform State Laws.

e. *Variations in Enactment of the Code*

The term, *Uniform Commercial Code*, is a misnomer at least to some degree. The various enacting jurisdictions have modified a number of individual Code sections with non-uniform variations from the Official Text.

Although this Nutshell refers where appropriate

to the revised 1972 and 1999 versions of the Code, it is impractical in a work of this nature to discuss individual state non-uniform modifications of particular Code sections of Article 9. The student of Article 9 who is concerned with the enactment in any particular jurisdiction should examine the specific enactment of that jurisdiction, to determine the existence of any non-uniform variations of individual sections from the Official Text of the Code sponsors.

f. Pre-Code Statutes Replaced by Code

The Uniform Commercial Code, in Articles other than Article 9 on Secured Transactions, replaces certain former uniform statutes. Article 9 itself also replaces some former statutes, including two former uniform statutes: the Uniform Trust Receipts Act and the Uniform Conditional Sales Act. The former uniform statute had rather widespread enactment; the latter uniform law on conditional sales had rather limited enactment.

A number of non-uniform state statutes covering secured transactions are also superseded by Article 9. Those include chattel mortgage laws enacted in virtually all states, non-uniform statutes governing conditional sales and other non-uniform statutes governing assignments of accounts receivable and factor's liens. The replaced statutes covered parts of the secured transactions area now covered comprehensively in Article 9.

§ 2. Purpose and Policy of Article 9

The 1999 version of Article 9 states that Article 9 may be cited as *Uniform Commercial Code – Secured Transactions.*

The aim of Article 9 is to provide a simple and unified structure within which the immense variety of present-day secured financing transactions can be carried out with less cost and more certainty than under pre-Code law. The general purpose of Article 9 is stated in the following material taken from the beginning of the Comment to 1972 § 9-101:

> This Article sets out a comprehensive scheme for the regulation of security interests in personal property and fixtures. It supersedes prior legislation dealing with such security devices as chattel mortgages, conditional sales, trust receipts, factor's liens and assignments of accounts receivable.

A similar statement is found in Comment 1 to 1999 § 9-101:

This Article supercedes former Uniform Commercial code (UCC) Article 9. As did its predecessor, it provides a comprehensive scheme for the regulation of security interests in personal property and fixtures.

Consumer installment sales and consumer loans present special problems of a nature which makes special regulation of them inappropriate in a general commercial codification. Many states now regulate such loans and sales under small loan acts, retail installment selling acts and the like. Note, however, that the 1999 Article 9 includes some special rules for "consumer goods," "consumer goods transactions," and "consumer transactions." See Comment 4(j) to 1999 § 9-101. Such special rules are discussed at various places in this Nutshell.

Under the Article, distinctions based on form or the label given a transaction are not controlling, unless the transaction takes the form of a "pledge"where the secured creditor is in possession of the collateral, or where the secured party takes "control" of some forms of collateral, or where the transaction produces a "purchase-money security interest" (all of which are discussed and defined elsewhere in this Nutshell), in which case the Article in some instances treats the transaction differently from other secured transactions. For some purposes there are distinctions based on the kind of property which constitutes the collateral – industrial and commercial equipment, business inventory, farm products, consumer goods, accounts receivable, documents of title and other intangibles. 1999 Article 9 also covers some additional kinds of property not covered in the 1972 version. Where appropriate, the Article states special rules applicable to financing transactions involving a particular type of property. Despite the statutory simplification, a greater degree of flexibility in the financing transaction is allowed than was possible under pre-Code law.

In both the 1972 and 1999 versions of Article 9, a more rational filing system replaces the former system of different files for each security device which is subject to filing requirements. Thus, not only is the information contained in the files made more accessible but the cost of procuring credit information and, incidentally, of maintaining the files, is greatly reduced.

The rules set out in Article 9 are principally concerned with two relationships: the secured creditor-debtor relationship and the relationship of the secured party to purchasers from and creditors of the debtor, that is, so-called third-party claimants.

§ 3. Secured Transactions Within Article 9

a. Definition of Secured Transaction

Article 9 of the Uniform Commercial Code primarily deals with *secured transactions in personal property*.

A *secured transaction* within the scope of Article 9 of the Code might be considered as any transaction which is *intended* to create in favor of one person a *security interest* in the *personal property* of someone else.

A secured transaction is one which produces for the benefit of the secured creditor a "lien" in the personal property of the debtor. The lien serves two functions for the creditor: (1) if the debtor defaults, *i.e.*, fails to pay the secured debt, the secured creditor may take possession of the personal property subject to the lien and use it to satisfy the debt; (2) if other creditors of or buyers from the debtor or a bankruptcy trustee assert a claim to the debtor's personal property, the creditor may be able to acquire a priority position through the lien. In these two regards, it may be said the personal property subject to the lien "secures" payment of the debt owed the secured creditor.

It must be kept in mind that Article 9 covers secured transactions for the most part *only in personal property*. While personal property within the scope of Article 9 includes *fixtures* (goods related to real estate), Article 9 does not apply to any real estate security interest, such as a mortgage or deed of trust. See § 5 of this chapter which lists excluded transactions.

A secured transaction in personal property ordinarily arises in two basic kinds of transactions: (1) a loan made to the owner of personal property which is secured by that property; and (2) a purchase of personal property on credit wherein the buyer gives a security interest in the purchased property either to the seller or to the person who makes a loan to enable the buyer to buy the property. This latter type of transaction creates a *purchase-money security interest*, similar to a conditional sale under pre-Code law. See discussion in § 9c(2) of this chapter.

Under Article 9, in any secured transaction, the property subject to the security interest (including accounts and chattel paper which have been sold) is referred to as the *collateral*. The 1999 Article 9 in § 9-102(a)(12) defines *collateral* as the property subject to a security interest or agricultural lien. The term "collateral" includes proceeds of collateral, accounts, chattel paper, payment intangibles, and promissory notes that have been sold, and goods that are the subject of a consignment.

The term "secured transaction" is not expressly defined in the Code, although there is a definition of the term "security interest" in pre-revision § 1-201(37) and revised § 1-201(b)(35), which basically defines that term as "an interest in personal property or fixtures which secures payment or performance of an obligation." The definition of "security interest" in pre-revision § 1-201(37) continues by considering whether certain transactions (such as a sale of goods with reservation of title in the seller, a lease of goods, or a consignment) may create a security interest. Similarly, see revised §§ 1-201(b)(35) and 1-203. Further discussion of "leases" and "consignments" occurs later in this Nutshell. See Chapter 2, § 6d, e.

Although the term "secured transaction" is not defined, 1999 § 9-109(a) declares that except for certain excluded transactions (see § 5 of this chapter), Article 9 applies to:

(1) a transaction, regardless of its form, that creates a security interest in personal property or fixtures by contract;

(2) an agricultural lien;

(3) a sale of accounts, chattel paper, payment intangibles, or promissory notes;

(4) a consignment;

(5) a security interest arising under certain provisions in the Articles on sales or leases of goods; and

(6) a security interest arising under certain provisions on bank deposits and collections or letters of credit.

In summary, a typical secured transaction might be outlined as involving (1) a debt, (2) a debtor, (3) a creditor or secured party, (4) personal property or fixtures making up the security or collateral, (5) an agreement which may take the form of a pledge, or control of the collateral by the secured party, or a security interest where the debtor is in possession.

Ordinarily, the debtor is the borrower on the security of the personal property collateral or the credit purchaser of the personal property that serves as the collateral. In certain instances, a third person may put up the collateral as security for the loan and the debtor may also be a third person serving as surety or guarantor of the obligation.

b. *Intention of the Parties*

A typical secured transaction is *consensual* in nature and requires that there be an *agreement* between the parties, the debtor and the secured party.

For example, such an agreement must be evidenced in an authenticated (signed) writing or other record and meet certain requirements unless the secured party has possession or control of the collateral. For discussion of the requirements of security agreements, see Chapter 2.

The basic test of the existence of a typical secured transaction in personal property usually is *whether the parties intended that a security interest exist*. Absent such an intention, Article 9 normally does not apply. However, without regard to intent to create a security interest, Article 9 applies to most sales of accounts, chattel paper, payment intangibles or promissory notes. See § 4 of this chapter.

It follows that Article 9 does not apply to a nonconsensual lien on personal property, such as a statutory lien, although the 1999 version of Article 9 includes coverage of agricultural liens for certain purposes.

Example 1. Dealer A had been financing the purchase of inventory for resale with finance company B. B notified A that B intended to terminate the financing relationship and A then negotiated with a second finance company C for the latter to take over A's inventory financing. While the negotiations were under way, A received a shipment of new inventory from the manufacturer.

The latter mistakenly billed the shipment to B and B mistakenly paid the manufacturer for the shipment. After the shipment arrived on A's premises, B discovered the mistake and took possession of the items shipped. There is no secured transaction between A and B covering that shipment and Article 9 does not apply.

Example 2. A entered into a contract for builder B to construct a building on A's premises. When B failed to complete construction, surety company C (which had issued a performance bond to B) took over and completed the work. After completion, A paid the amount due for the work to C which asserted its common-law right of subrogation to amounts that had been due from A to B under the contract. D, the trustee in bankruptcy of B, claimed the amount paid by A to C on the ground that C had not taken action under Article 9 to perfect its security interest in that amount. There is no secured transaction, since C's right to payment by A arose under common-law rights of subrogation. Thus, C is entitled to retain the payment even though C did not perfect a security interest under Article 9.

c. Additional Coverage in 1999 Article 9

The 1999 Article 9 expanded the coverage of

kinds of property subject to secured transactions in certain respects. Coverage in the 1999 version includes (as covered in Comment 4a to 1999 § 9-101): deposit accounts, sales of payment intangibles and promissory notes, healthcare-insurance receivables, nonpossessory statutory agricultural liens, consignments, supporting obligations and property securing rights to payment, commercial tort claims, transfers by States and governmental units of States, nonassignable general intangibles, promissory notes, healthcare-insurance receivables, and letter-of-credit rights.

§ 4. Sales of Accounts, Chattel Paper, Payment Intangibles, or Promissory Notes

The 1999 Article 9 in § 9-109(a)(3) indicates the Article applies to a sale of accounts or chattel paper and additionally applies to a sale of payment intangibles or promissory notes. The reason for the rule subjecting such sales to Article 9 is that commercial financing on the basis of accounts, chattel paper and similar property is often conducted such that the distinction between a security transfer and a sale is blurred, with the buyer treated as a secured party and the buyer's interest treated as a security interest. See Comment 4 to 1999 § 9-109. The definitions of the terms "account," "chattel paper," "payment intangibles," and "promissory note" are considered later in this chapter. See § 7b, c and e.

Comment 4 to 1999 § 9-109 specifically states that the approach treating sales of accounts and chattel paper "generally has been successful in avoiding difficult problems of distinguishing between transactions in which a receivable secures an obligation and those in which the receivable has been sold outright. In many commercial financing transactions the distinction is blurred." Comment 4 continues by noting the expansion of 1999 § 9-109(a)(3) to include the sale of a "payment intangible" and the sale of a "promissory note."

Although, as stated above, 1999 Article 9 applies to sales of accounts, chattel paper, payment intangibles or promissory notes, certain sales or assignments are completely excluded from coverage under Article 9. See discussion in § 5g of this chapter.

§ 5. Excluded Transactions

There are a number of transactions that are excluded from Article 9 coverage. 1999 § 9-109(c) speaks of certain transactions that are not within Article 9 and 1999 § 9-109(d) lists other transactions to which Article 9 does not apply.

(1) Certain transactions subject to federal law are at least to some extent excluded. 1999 § 9-109(c)(1) declares that Article 9 does not apply to the extent that a statute, regulation, or treaty of the United States preempts Article 9. It is clear in the 1999 version that the exclusion applies only where there is federal preemption and not to areas where federal law merely deals with some subject matter also within Article 9. The important thing to remember is that certain matters must be researched on a federal as well as a state level. For example, where ship mortgages, aircraft titles, patents and copyrights, railroad equipment and some interstate commercial vehicles are involved, federal law may be preemptive.

(2) Under 1999 § 9-109(c)(2), Article 9 does not apply where another statute of the enacting state governs the creation, perfection, priority, or enforcement of a security interest created by that state or a governmental unit of that state. 1999 § 9-109(c)(3) also states that Article 9 does not apply to the extent that a statute of another state or county or governmental unit of the same, other than a statute generally applicable to security interests (such as Article 9 of another state), expressly governs creation, perfection, priority or enforcement of a

security interest created by the other state, county, or governmental unit. In other words, Article 9 of the enacting state defers to statutes of another state or foreign country only to the extent that the other statutes contain rules applicable specifically to security interests created by the particular governmental unit of the other jurisdiction.

(3) 1999 § 9-109(c)(4) states that Article 9 does not apply to the extent the rights of a transferee beneficiary or nominated person under a letter of credit are independent and superior under the letter-of-credit Article (§ 5-114) dealing with assignment of proceeds of a letter of credit.

(4) Article 9 does not apply to a landlord's lien under 1999 § 9-109(d)(1) except for an agricultural lien. Agricultural liens are within 1999 Article 9 for certain purposes. See 1999 § 9-109(a)(2).

(5) Article 9 does not apply to a lien given by statute or rule of law for services or materials under 1999 § 9-109(d)(2) except for an agricultural lien. Those liens are often referred to as "artisan's liens." Another provision (1999 § 9-333) sets forth rules of priority of any lien for services or materials as against an Article 9 security interest.

(6) Transfer or assignment of a claim for wages, salary or other compensation of an employee is

excluded from Article 9 under 1999 § 9-109(d)(3). Such assignments are regulated by other federal and state statutes and present important social issues that other law addresses.

(7) Article 9 does not apply to certain sales or assignments of accounts, chattel paper, payment intangibles or promissory notes that by their nature have nothing to do with commercial financing transactions. Thus, such sales as part of the complete sale of a business are excluded. Assignments of such for the purpose of collection only are similarly excluded. A transfer or assignment of a right of payment under a contract to an assignee that is also obligated to perform under the contract is also excluded. Finally, a transfer or assignment of a single account, payment intangible, or promissory note to an assignee in full or partial satisfaction of a preexisting indebtedness is excluded. See 1999 § 9-104(d)(4)-(7).

In short, using accounts as an example, if a business is sold to another person who takes over the seller's accounts, Article 9 does not apply. If a business turns over overdue accounts to a collection agency, Article 9 does not apply. If a contract is assigned to another person who is to take over the assignor's obligations and also to receive the assignor's rights to payment, Article 9 does not apply. If a business owes money to another and assigns to the other person the proceeds of a single account owed to the business by a third person, Article 9 does not apply.

(8) Article 9 does not apply with respect to a transfer of an interest in or assignment of a claim under a policy of insurance. Such transactions are also special and do not fit easily into a general secured transactions statute. However, Article 9 provisions apply with respect to proceeds and priorities in proceeds of insurance policies. See 1999 § 9-109(a)(8). For example, if an automobile that is collateral in a secured transaction is destroyed in an accident, the secured party has a security interest in the payment made to the policyholder by the insurance company under a "collision" insurance policy.

While Article 9 generally excludes transfer of an interest in or assignment of a claim under a policy of insurance, in 1999 § 9-109(d)(8) there is an exception for an assignment by or to a healthcare provider of a healthcare receivable and any subsequent assignment of a right to payment in the 1999 enactment. Certain 1999 provisions apply to healthcare receivables.

(9) Article 9 does not apply to a right represented by a judgment other than a judgment

taken on a right to payment that was collateral under 1999 § 9-109(d)(9).

(10) Article 9 does not apply to a right of recoupment or setoff under 1999 § 9-109(d)(10) subject to two exceptions. One of the exceptions applies to a setoff against a deposit account that is collateral. The second recognizes the right of an obligor on an account, chattel paper, or general intangible to raise claims and defenses against an assignee (secured party). See Comment 14 to 1999 § 9-109.

"Recoupment" is the legal ability to subtract from any payment due the amount the person trying to collect the debt (or that person's predecessor) happens to owe the debtor. "Setoff" is a common law right that allows parties to net out mutual debts. In essence, a setoff may occur where two parties are debtors to each other as to separate credit transactions and one party defaults. The other party may then reduce the defaulted obligation by reducing their debt to the defaulting party.

(11) According to 1999 § 9-109(d)(11), Article 9 does not apply to the creation or transfer of an interest in or lien on real estate, including a lease or rents thereunder. However, a security interest in fixtures is within the scope of Article 9. Provision also is made for fixture filings. The 1999 provision

also permits a security agreement covering both real and personal property and permits certain liens (in 1999 § 9-203 and 9-308) on real property.

Issues have arisen as to whether a mortgagee's interest (the note payable to the mortgagee and real estate mortgage which secures it) when used as collateral falls within the scope of Article 9. It appears when the note and mortgage are used as collateral to secure payment of an extension of credit to the mortgagee, the transaction falls within the scope of Article 9. However, should the mortgagor use its interest in the real estate as collateral for an extension of credit, the transaction does not fall within the scope of Article 9. Similar issues have arisen regarding land sale contracts. There is a split of authority regarding whether a vendor's interest when used as collateral is within the scope of Article 9. Most probably, the vendee's interest when used as collateral in a transaction would involve a transaction outside the scope of Article 9.

(12) A transfer of a tort claim is excluded in 1999 § 9-109(d)(12). However, it excludes only tort claims that are other than "commercial tort" claims. 1999 Article 9 applies to commercial tort claims as well as assignments of tort claims that constitute proceeds of other collateral (such as a right to payment for destruction of inventory serving as

collateral).

(13) Deposit accounts, when used as collateral, are within 1999 Article 9 except under § 9-109(d)(13) which excludes an assignment of a deposit account in a consumer transaction. In other words, nonconsumer deposit accounts, when used as collateral, fall within 1999 Article 9's scope. Proceeds and priorities in proceeds of both consumer and nonconsumer accounts are within 1999 Article 9's scope.

§ 6. Parties to Secured Transaction

a. Debtor

The principal parties to a secured transaction are the *debtor* and the *secured party*, terms which are defined in the Code.

The 1999 UCC in § 9-102(a)(28) defines "debtor" as (A) a person having an interest, other than a security interest or other lien in the collateral, whether or not that person is an obligor; (B) a seller of accounts, chattel paper, payment intangibles, or promissory notes; or (C) a consignee.

Comment 2 to 1999 § 9-102 explains the definition, which also introduces the terms "obligor" and "secondary obligor" absent from the 1972

Article 9. In most instances, the "debtor" is one who has a stake in the proper enforcement of the security interest by virtue of a non-lien interest in the property, usually an ownership interest. In most instances, the "debtor" is also an "obligor." That term is defined in 1999 § 9-102(a)(59) and usually is the person who owes the debt. A "secondary obligor" is defined in 1999 § 9-102(a)(71) and usually indicates a person who is a surety or guarantor of the debt.

The 1999 definition of "debtor" also includes a seller of accounts, chattel paper, payment intangibles or promissory notes. The 1999 definition further defines a "debtor" as including a consignee of goods. 1999 Article 9 removes from the Sales Article 2 most aspects of consignment sales and transfers such consignment transactions to 1999 Article 9.

Other terms that may be synonymous with the term "debtor" would include "borrower" or "buyer." A "buyer" might include a person who purchases goods on credit and gives a "purchase-money security interest" in the goods for the unpaid price.

b. *Secured Party*

The term "secured party" is defined in 1999 § 9-

102(a)(72) as a person in whose favor a security interest is created or provided for under a security agreement, whether or not any obligation to be secured is outstanding; a person that holds an agricultural lien; a consignor; a person to which accounts, chattel paper, payment intangibles, or promissory notes have been sold; a trustee, indenture trustee, agent, collateral agent, or other representative in whose favor a security interest or agricultural lien is created or provided for; or a person that holds a security interest arising under certain provisions of Articles 2, 2A, 4 and 5.

The references to a person holding an agricultural lien and to a consignor are new as contrasted with the revised 1972 Article 9, the latter reference again recognizing the transfer of much of the law of consignment transactions from Article 2 to 1999 Article 9. The references to certain provisions of Articles 2, 2A, 4 and 5 recognize certain security interests given in sections of those Articles but do not require a security agreement or filing.

Other terms which might apply to a "secured party" include "lender," "obligee," "financer" or "seller." The latter term would include a person who sells goods on credit and takes a purchase-money security interest for the unpaid price.

c. Account Debtor

Still another term used in Article 9 is "account debtor," defined as "the person who is obligated on an account, chattel paper or general intangible." See 1999 § 9-102(a)(3). The term does not include persons obligated to pay a negotiable instrument, even if the instrument constitutes part of chattel paper.

Example 1. A buys widgets from B on credit and gives B a security interest in the widgets for the unpaid price by means of a signed security agreement and a promissory note. B assigns the security agreement and indorses the note to C, as security for a debt owed by B to C. C is the assignee and secured party, B is the assignor and debtor and A is the account debtor. The note and security agreement together are chattel paper.

Example 2. B sells widgets to A on open account and B assigns the account due from A to C as security for a debt owed by B to C. C is the assignee and secured party, B is the assignor and debtor and A is the account debtor.

Comment 5b to 1999 § 9-102 states that the rules in various provisions of 1999 Article 9 dealing with an "account debtor" do not apply where an assignment of chattel paper is evidenced by a negotiable instrument.   Rather, the assignee's rights are governed by UCC Article 3.

§ 7. Collateral: Definition and Classes

Collateral is defined in 1999 § 9-102(a)(12) as the property subject to a security interest or agricultural lien. The term includes: proceeds to which a security interest attaches; accounts, chattel paper, payment intangibles, and promissory notes that have been sold; and goods that are the subject of a consignment.

There are different classes of collateral under Article 9. The Article frequently treats secured transactions differently depending upon the class of collateral involved.   Thus, it is important to understand which class of collateral is involved in a particular secured transaction.

"Goods" are defined in 1999 § 9-102(a)(44). The definition is rather lengthy. It includes all things that are movable when a security interest attaches. The definition includes fixtures, standing timber to be cut and removed under a conveyance or contract for sale, the unborn young of animals, and crops. Crops include those produced on trees, vines, or bushes. The 1999 definition also adds as goods manufactured homes.   "Goods" in the 1999 definition also includes a computer program embedded in goods and any supporting information provided in connection with a transaction relating to the program if (i) the program is associated with the goods in such a manner that it customarily is considered part of the goods, or (ii) by becoming the owner of the goods, a person acquires a right to use the program in connection with the goods. The term does not include a computer program embedded in goods that consist solely of the medium in which the program is embedded. "Goods" does not include accounts, chattel paper, commercial tort claims, deposit accounts, documents, general intangibles, instruments, investment property, letter-of-credit rights, letters of credit, money, or oil, gas, or other minerals before extraction.

a. Goods.

Goods are classified as follows:

(1) *Consumer goods* are goods used or bought for use primarily for personal, family or household purposes. See 1999 § 9-102(a)(23).

Example. Homeowner gives a security interest in their household furniture to Secured Party.

(2) *Farm products* under 1999 § 9-102(a)(34) are

"goods, other than standing timber, with respect to which the debtor is engaged in a farming operation and which are crops grown, growing, or to be grown, including crops produced on trees, vines, and bushes, and aquatic goods produced in aquacultural operations. Farm products would also include livestock, born or unborn, including aquatic goods produced in aquacultural operations and supplies used or produced in a farming operation or products of crops or livestock in their unmanufactured states."

The 1999 definition expands the 1972 definition to cover crops growing on trees, vines and bushes and "aquatic goods," such as fish on a fish farm or hatchery or cultivated oysters. It is stated that standing timber is not a "farm product." Presumably, standing timber to be cut is "inventory."

(3) *Inventory* under 1999 § 9-102(a)(48) is defined as goods, other than farm products, which are leased by a person as lessor; are held by a person for sale or lease or to be furnished under a contract of service; are furnished by a person under a contract of service; or consist of raw materials, work in process, or materials used or consumed in a business.

(4) *Equipment* under 1999 § 9-102(a)(33) is merely defined as goods other than inventory, farm

products, or consumer goods.

Example. Manufacturer gives a security interest in the machinery used in the factory to Secured Party.

Comment 4a to 1999 § 9-102 notes:

> "The classes of goods are mutually exclusive. For example, the same property cannot simultaneously be both equipment and inventory. In borderline cases – a physician's car or a farmer's truck that might be either consumer goods or equipment – the principal use to which the property is put is determinative. Goods can fall into different classes at different times. For example, a radio may be inventory in the hands of a dealer and consumer goods in the hands of a consumer."

It is stated that goods are "equipment" if they do not fall into another category.

(5) *Fixtures* are goods that have become so related to particular real estate or real property that an interest in them arises under real estate law. See 1999 § 9-102(a)(41). However, no security interest arises under Article 9 in ordinary building materials incorporated into an improvement on land. See 1999 § 9-334(a).

In short, real estate law governs whether goods are fixtures; but when they are fixtures, property rights are governed both by real estate law and the law of personal property.

Examples of fixtures. A furnace affixed to a house or other building; counters permanently affixed to the floor of a store; a sprinkler system installed in a building.

Note as to fixtures that as personal property under the Code, fixtures are also either consumer goods or equipment. It is difficult to conceive of goods being both inventory and fixtures, since they are not normally affixed to real estate while being held for sale in the ordinary course of business. Crops are farm products but are not fixtures, even though they have a relation to real estate. Personal property that is attached to realty but is easily removable (such as carpeting tacked to a floor) is not a fixture.

(6) *Accessions* are goods that are physically united with other goods in such a manner that the identity of the original goods is not lost. See 1999 § 9-102(a)(1). But easily removable goods installed on other goods (such as tires mounted on the wheels of an automobile) usually are not accessions.

b. Indispensable Paper.

This expression does not appear in the Code as such. Indispensable paper covers various categories of paper which are negotiable or which are to some extent dealt with as if negotiable. This category has also been referred to as *semi-intangibles* or *commercial specialties*.

(1) *Document* means document of title, such as a bill of lading or warehouse receipt. See 1999 § 9-102(a)(30). See also the Article 1 definitions of *bill of lading* in pre-revision § 1-201(6) and revised § 1-201(b)(6), *document of title* in pre-revision § 1-201(15) and revised § 1-201(b)(16), and *warehouse receipt* in pre-revision § 1-201(45) and revised § 1-201(b)(42).

(2) *Instrument* means most commonly a negotiable instrument (draft, check, certificate of deposit or note). See 1999 § 9-102(a)(47). Note that "instrument" does not include "investment property."

(3) *Investment property* most importantly means an investment security such as stocks, bonds or the like but also includes commodity accounts and contracts. See 1999 § 9-102(a) (49). An investment security can be certificated or uncertificated. See § 9a(3) of this chapter for discussion.

(4) *Chattel paper* generally means a record or records that evidence both a monetary obligation and a security interest in or lease of specific goods. When a transaction is evidenced both by such a security agreement or a lease and by an instrument or series of instruments, the group of records taken together constitutes chattel paper. See 1999 § 9-102(a)(11).

Example. Dealer sells a tractor to Farmer on a conditional sales contract or a purchase-money security interest. The conditional sales contract is a *security agreement*, Farmer is the *debtor*, Dealer is the *secured party* and the tractor is the kind of *collateral* defined as *equipment*. Dealer then transfers the contract to their bank either by outright sale or to secure a loan. Since the conditional sales contract is a security agreement relating to specific equipment, the conditional sales contract is now the type of collateral called *chattel paper*. In this transaction between Dealer and their bank, the bank is the *secured party*, Dealer is the *debtor*, and Farmer is the *account debtor*. *If a promissory note is included with the conditional sales contract or security agreement, the writings taken together are chattel paper.*

c. Intangibles.

This type of collateral is purely intangible, that is, intangibles not evidenced by an indispensable writing but which may be the subject of a commercial financing transaction.

(1) *Account* generally means any right to payment for goods sold or leased or for services rendered which is not evidenced by an instrument or chattel paper, whether or not it has been earned by performance. This covers the ordinary account receivable. See 1999 § 9-102(a)(2).

Example. Dealer sells goods to buyers on open account (on an unsecured basis) wherein the buyers have 60 days in which to pay. Dealer assigns the accounts to Bank either by outright sale or to secure a loan. In this transaction between Dealer and Bank, Bank is the *secured party*, Dealer is the *debtor* and the several buyers are the *account debtors*.

(2) *General intangibles* means any personal property (including things in action) other than goods, accounts, chattel paper, documents, instruments and money, i.e., purely intangible collateral which is not an account.

Examples. Goodwill, literary rights, rights to performance, and also copyrights, trademarks and patents if not excluded from the applicability of

Article 9 as security interests subject to any statute of the United States. See 1999 § 9-109(a)(42).

d. Proceeds.

Proceeds primarily includes whatever is received upon the sale, lease, license, exchange or other disposition of collateral or proceeds. Money, checks, deposit accounts, and the like are cash proceeds. All other proceeds are non-cash proceeds. See 1999 § 9-102(a)(64).

Example. Dealer gives a security interest in their inventory to Bank. Buyer buys item from Dealer's inventory and makes a cash down payment and trades in an old car. Buyer pays the balance by check. The cash, trade-in car and check are all proceeds of the inventory collateral. Note that when the used car traded in is itself sold again by Dealer, other proceeds arise from that sale and might be considered as *proceeds of proceeds* in connection with the original sale of the new car.

e. Other kinds of collateral.

Other kinds of collateral also referred to in the 1999 version of Article 9 include:

(1) *Timber to be cut*. 1999 §§ 9-102(a)(44)(ii) and 9-502.

(2) *Minerals (including oil and gas), also termed "as-extracted" collateral.* 1999 §§ 9-502, 9-301(4), 9-102(a)(6) and 9-102(a)(44).

(3) *Money*. 1999 §§ 9-312, 9-313.

(4) *Deposit accounts* (including nonconsumer bank accounts). 1999 § 9-102(a)(29).

(5) *Payment intangibles* (a general intangible under which the account debtor's principal obligation is a monetary obligation). 1999 § 9-102(a)(61).

(6) *Health-care insurance receivable* (essentially an interest or claim under a health insurance policy). 1999 § 9-102(a)(46).

(7) *Supporting obligations* (essentially a letter-of-credit right or secondary obligation that supports payment of an account, chattel paper and document, a general intangible, an instrument, or investment property). 1999 § 9-102(a)(77).

(8) *Commercial tort claims* (essentially where the claimant is an organization or the claim is business related). 1999 § 9-102(a)(13).

(9) *Letter-of-credit right* (essentially a right to

payment under a letter of credit). 1999 § 9-102(a)
(51).

§ 8. Attachment and Perfection of Security
    Interest

Article 9 of the Uniform Commercial Code
speaks in terms of two different concepts in connection with a security interest in personal property
collateral: *attachment of a security interest* and
perfection of a security interest.

Attachment of a security interest might be considered as equivalent to creation of a security
interest; in other words, unless there is attachment of
a security interest, there is no security interest
whatever. However, once a security interest has
attached, the secured party can enforce the interest
and realize on the collateral, at least as against the
debtor.

The additional step of *perfection of a security
interest* is necessary when the secured party seeks to
enforce the interest against third persons who assert
interests in the collateral, such as other creditors of
the debtor, a bankruptcy trustee should the debtor
file bankruptcy, or persons to whom the collateral is
transferred. Where perfection takes place, the
security interest is enforceable, not only against the

debtor, but also against most (though not all) third persons with claims against the collateral.

For discussion of attachment of a security interest, see Chapters 2 and 3.

For discussion of perfection of a security interest, see Chapters 4, 5 and 6.

§ 9. Particular Security Devices

Article 9 does not place great emphasis on the form a secured transaction takes, with the exception of when the secured party has possession of the collateral (commonly referred to as a "pledge"), when the secured party has "control" of the collateral, and when a transaction produces by its form a "purchase-money security interest." However, it is helpful from a practical standpoint to have some understanding of how secured transactions have been and still are structured.

a. *Pledge or Possessory Security Interest.*

(1) *General Characteristics.* A *pledge*, considered as a transaction, is a bailment or delivery of goods or property by way of security for a debt or engagement, or as security for the performance of an

act. Another definition is that a *pledge* is a security interest in a chattel or in an intangible represented by an indispensable instrument (such as formal, written evidence of an interest in an intangible so representing the intangible that the enjoyment, transfer, or enforcement of the intangible depends upon possession of the instrument), the interest being created by a bailment for the purpose of securing the payment of a debt or the performance of some other duty. See Restatement, Security, § 1.

It is necessary not only that there be an agreement to pledge, *but also that there be delivery of possession* to the pledgee or secured party (or in some instances to a third person acting for the secured party). *There is no pledge where the debtor remains in possession*, even where they purportedly act as agent for the secured party.

The earliest form of secured transaction in personal property was the pledge and it is still used to secure loans in situations where the item pledged does not have to be retained by the borrower. Pledges may be used to secure loans on such valuables as jewelry. Pledges are often used where the collateral consists of *instruments*, such as promissory notes, or some form of investment property such as stock certificates, bonds and the like, or *negotiable documents,* such as bills of lading or warehouse receipts.

On the other hand, a pledge is impossible with respect to complete intangibles which do not consist of documents or instruments that confer property rights on one in possession. This is made clear in 1999 § 9-313 which permits a security interest to be perfected by taking of possession only when the collateral is goods, instruments, negotiable documents, money or tangible chattel paper. Accounts, commercial tort claims, deposit accounts, investment property, letter-of-credit rights, letters of credit, money, oil, gas or other minerals before extraction are excluded. See Comment 1 to 1999 § 9-313. Under the 1999 Code, a secured party may perfect a security interest in certificated securities by taking delivery of the certificated security. See 1999 § 9-313(a) and Comment 6; see also § 8-301. Thus, a pledge is meaningless with respect to accounts or general intangibles, although such items of personal property may be assigned.

Under the 1999 Code, no record (*i.e.*, writing) of the security agreement is necessary when the collateral is pledged or in the possession of the secured party. Also, under the 1999 Code, a security interest is perfected without filing when the collateral is in the possession of the secured party. See 1999 §§ 9-203 and 9-313.

If a secured party has an unperfected security interest in collateral in the debtor's possession (as where the secured party failed to file a financing statement), the secured party nonetheless obtains a perfected security interest if they repossess the collateral after the debtor's default. Such a secured party who has repossessed has all the rights and duties of a pledgee or secured party in possession. See 1999 § 9-601(b) and Comment 4.

(2) *Field Warehousing.* A security interest may be perfected under the Code without filing where the collateral is in the possession of the secured party. See 1999 §§ 9-203 and 9-313. However, *either the secured party or a third person acting for the secured party must be in possession.* If the debtor is in possession or has ready access to the pledged property, the security interest remains unperfected; there is no pledge.

There is a special form of pledge transaction known as field warehousing. This is an arrangement whereby a pledgor may have necessary access to the pledged goods, while the goods are actually in the custody and control of a third person, *acting as a warehouseman on the pledgor's premises.*

Field warehousing is often employed as a security device in inventory financing where the financer or secured party desires to maintain close control over the borrower's inventory and have the advantages of being a pledgee of the property. The device is employed in financing manufacturers or wholesalers in seasonal industries (for example, a manufacturer of Christmas tree ornaments). The device is also useful where the manufactured products must be aged or cured or where they are accumulated over a period of time and then disposed of all at once.

The field warehousing operation is carried out through the financer's employment of a warehouseman who leases space on the borrower's premises at a nominal rate and sets up a warehouse in that space where the borrower's unsold inventory is stored. Warehouse receipts are usually issued by the warehouseman covering the goods in storage and those documents are delivered to the financer. Thus, the goods in the field warehouse are in effect pledged to the financer.

The major difficulty under pre-Code law with field warehousing was that such a transaction was often not regarded as a proper pledge where the borrower was permitted too easy access to the goods. For effective field warehousing, it is necessary that the space for the field warehouse be effectively segregated from the remainder of the borrower's premises. This may be done by taking a room that can be locked or other space that can be partitioned off, with access denied any unauthorized person. The field warehouse company usually employs a custodian, and the custodian is often a former employee of the borrower (such as a shipping clerk) who is placed on the warehouseman's payroll.

Many of the problems as to the effectiveness of the field warehousing operation arise from the fact that the custodian (as a former and possible future employee of the borrower) is likely to allow the borrower too ready access to the goods, thus destroying the effectiveness of the transaction as a pledge.

A secured party under the Code who desires to conduct a field warehouse on the borrower's premises may avoid the risk inherent in too loose supervision of the warehouse operations by filing a financing statement under Article 9. In this manner, the secured party retains a perfected security interest in the warehoused goods, even if the field warehouse operation is not properly conducted. In other words, the secured party can maintain as much control as is desired through the field warehouse; yet the secured party need not risk the consequences of a lapse of control. They can file under Article 9 and have a perfected security interest, regardless of whether they maintain tight or loose control over the borrower's inventory.

In fact, it would seem advisable to file under

Article 9, even where the field warehousing operation is properly conducted. In particular, filing is advisable if it is contemplated that periodic release to the borrower of the warehoused goods is necessary. Moreover, filing may be helpful where any question of the propriety of the disposition of the goods by the secured party after the borrower's default is at issue.

(3) *Investment Property.* The 1972 version of Article 9 was significantly amended regarding security interests in investment securities and the like in 1994. These amendments changed the method by which secured transactions in such collateral are structured.

The 1999 version of Article 9 does not substantially change how a secured transaction should be structured to obtain perfection of a security interest in investment property. As to perfection of a security interest in investment property, see discussion at Chapter 4, § 4(b).

The above-mentioned 1994 amendments, which involved changes both to Article 8 and to the 1972 Article 9, dealt not only with stocks and bonds represented by physical pieces of paper, known as *certificated securities* [see § 8-102(a)(4)], but also with similar rights against an issuing corporation that are evidenced by a registration in a computer at the corporation, known as *uncertificated securities* [see § 8-102(a)(18)]. The amendments also recognized the current method of holding securities in an account with a stockbroker in which the stockholder's ownership is reflected merely by a bookkeeping entry in the stockbroker's records, known as a *securities entitlement* [see § 8-102(a)(17)]. The 1994 amendments to Article 9 combined these methods of owning securities with similar ownership rights in commodity contracts and accounts. The 1994 Code referred to all such property as *investment property*. See § 9-115 (1972 version as amended in 1994). The 1999 Article 9 continues use of the same term. See § 9-102(a)(49).

There are essentially two methods of structuring a secured transaction in investment property. One method does not involve taking possession or control of the investment property by the secured party; rather the secured party, after attaching the security interest, will file a financing statement. See 1999 § 9-312(a). Under the second method, the secured party takes "control" of the investment property. See 1999 § 9-314(a). There are different ways to take control of the investment property. For example, a secured party has control over a certificated security by taking possession of it, along with any necessary indorsements. See §§ 8-106(a), (b) and 8-301(a).

b. Chattel Mortgage

At common law, the only known security devices were the mortgage of real estate and the pledge of chattels. Obviously, a pledge was of little value, where, by the nature of the transaction, it was necessary that the debtor have possession of the collateral. It necessarily followed that the device of recording a mortgage could be utilized for tangible personal property, as well as real estate.

In the 19th century, a number of statutes were enacted validating chattel mortgages upon the filing or recording of such instruments at a local public office. The style of such a transaction itself was apparently borrowed from the concept of recording a mortgage on real estate. Such chattel mortgage filing or recording statutes persisted, often in rather fragmentary form, until replaced by Article 9 of the Code.

The usual characteristics of a chattel mortgage were a debt owed the mortgagee by the mortgagor and an agreement subjecting specified personal property as security for the debt. By statute, such chattel mortgages were generally declared void against such persons as other secured or lien creditors of the borrower or purchasers of the collateral, unless the mortgage was filed or recorded as prescribed by statute or unless the mortgagee took possession of the collateral.

In general, the chattel mortgage instrument itself had to be filed or recorded and had to describe the property covered and the obligation or debt secured by the mortgage. Some pre-Code statutes required that the chattel mortgage be signed by the mortgagor and be witnessed or acknowledged before a notary. Some other statutes required inclusion of a sworn affidavit that the mortgage had been given in good faith or that it had been given for good consideration.

A chattel mortgage may still be used under the Uniform Commercial Code if it complies with the relatively simple Code requirements necessary in connection with any security agreement, and a chattel mortgage may be filed under the Code if it complies with the relatively simple requirements as to form for a filed financing statement.

c. Conditional Sale

(1) *General Characteristics.* Another form of security device which developed during the 19th century was the so-called *conditional sale* or sale with reservation of title in the seller. Such a sale might be made conditional on the occurrence or non-occurrence of some event, and thus not final until the

described event had taken place or had not. But the term *conditional sale* (also sometimes called a "retain title" sale) came to mean a sale in which title was reserved in the seller until the purchase price had been paid in full. Thus, a seller might sell goods on installment credit and, by agreement, retain title to the goods until all installments were paid by the buyer. The agreement might permit the seller to repossess the goods upon any default on the part of the buyer, such as delay in paying a due installment of the price.

In most states under pre-Code law, conditional sales were distinguished from chattel mortgages. The conditional sale device could be used only by a seller of the goods and could not be used by one lending on the security of goods. (A chattel mortgage could be used for either an installment sale of goods or a loan secured by goods.) However, conditional sales were considered desirable because at common law such a sale was effective to retain title in the seller without the necessity of filing or recording, even when the buyer had possession. Some states permitted conditional sales without filing or recording even up to the time of enactment of the Code. However, other states enacted the Uniform Conditional Sales Act or a non-uniform statute which required the filing or recording of conditional sales transactions in order to permit the unpaid seller to retain rights to the goods as against the buyer's creditors.

Transactions under the Uniform Commercial Code may be cast in the form of conditional sales, and a conditional sales agreement may serve as a security agreement if it meets the rather simple Code requirements for such an agreement. A transaction in the form of a conditional sale under the Code gives rise to a purchase-money security interest, which is discussed below.

(2) Purchase-Money Security Interest

To some extent, some of the pre-Code functional concepts of conditional sales have been retained in the Article 9 provisions dealing with purchase-money security interests.

The 1999 Article 9 defines purchase-money security interest at 1999 § 9-103, which indicates that "purchase-money collateral" means goods or software that secures a purchase-money obligation and then provides that a purchase-money obligation is one that an obligor incurs as all or part of the price of the collateral or for value given to enable the debtor to acquire rights in or use of the collateral if the value is in fact so used. See 1999 § 9-103(a). That section then applies these definitions to purchase-money security interests in goods [1999

§ 9-103(b)], software [1999 § 9-103(c)], and to consignors [1999 § 9-103(d)].

A secured transaction that produces a purchase-money security interest is probably the most important and most common of secured transactions under Article 9.   It gives the secured party certain advantages not given with respect to a non-purchase-money security interest. For one thing, a secured party with a purchase-money security interest has twenty days under the 1999 Code after the debtor obtains the collateral to file, and such filing relates back to the time the debtor obtained possession for most purposes. See 1999 §§ 9-317(e) and 9-324(a). However, the twenty-day period does not apply to inventory under 1999 § 9-324. Such a purchase-money secured party also has, if their interest is timely perfected, priority over other perfected non-purchase-money security interests. See 1999 § 9-324(a) and (b).

The Code follows pre-Code law of many states which permitted conditional sales without filing by permitting perfection of a purchase-money security interest in consumer goods without filing. Thus, many secured transactions of relatively large total volume but of relatively small individual dollar amounts are perfected without filing under 1999 § 9-309(1).

However, filing or compliance with certificate-of-title laws is necessary with respect to motor vehicles. See 1999 §§ 9-309(1)and 9-311(a), (b). 1999 § 9-334 also requires a fixture filing to secure priority over certain conflicting real estate interests in some cases where consumer goods are fixtures. See also 1999 § 9-309, Comment 3.

Example 1. A desires to buy widgets from B and enters into an agreement with B whereby A pays $100 cash as a down payment and agrees to pay $100 a month for 12 months. B retains a security interest in the widgets which are collateral for A's obligation to make the monthly payments. B has taken a purchase-money security interest in the widgets. If B assigns the interest to C, C also acquires a purchase-money security interest in the widgets.

Example 2. A desires to buy widgets from B for a price of $1,200. A borrows $1,100 from C and, with the borrowed sum and $100 of their own, purchases the widgets from B. A agrees to pay $100 a month for 12 months for the loan and also gives C a security interest in the widgets as collateral for A's obligation to make the monthly payments. C has taken a purchase-money security interest in the widgets, even though C did not sell the widgets to A. C has a purchase-money security interest whether they make the loan by directly paying $1,100 to the seller B or whether C advances the $1,100 to A and A applies that sum, plus $100 of their own, to purchase the widgets from B.

Example 3. A borrows money from B and gives B a security interest in widgets already owned by A as collateral for A's obligation to repay the loan. B does not have a purchase-money security interest in the widgets.

d. Other Security Devices

(1) *Trust Receipts.* A form of financing was developed to finance importers of goods and automobile and appliance dealers by the use of "trust receipts." Under this form of financing, an importer or dealer might finance their inventory by delivering to the lender a paper called a "trust receipt," which recognized that title to the goods received by the borrower was in the lender, while the borrower was in possession. This form of financing was often legally unsatisfactory under pre-Code chattel mortgage and conditional sales statutes; but its effectiveness was made clear under the Uniform Trust Receipts Act. Under that Act, a lender could obtain a security interest in inventory items in the borrower's possession by obtaining signed trust

receipts for such items from the borrower and by filing a rather simple form of statement (similar to an Article 9 financing statement) in a central state office. Financing using the trust receipt device may also be carried on under Article 9 of the Code.

(2) *Factor's Liens*. Another method of inventory financing, used to finance shifting stocks of small items of inventory, was by use of a device whereby a factor (lender) had by agreement a lien on inventory in the borrower's possession. Some states had non-uniform statutes permitting the factor to perfect a lien by filing a notice of lien in a public office.

(3) *Assignments of Accounts Receivable*. When inventory is sold by a manufacturer, wholesaler or other seller, it is often sold on open account, thereby creating an "account receivable." In many instances, such accounts may be assigned to a lender as security for advances made to the borrower (the manufacturer or seller of inventory). In some instances, such accounts were sold outright to a factor. Because of difficulty in effectively financing such accounts under pre-Code law, so-called non-uniform "assignment of accounts receivable" statutes were enacted in some but not all states. Some of the statutes provided for the filing of a notice of assignment in a public office. The Code clearly

permits the financing of accounts and sets forth the effect of assignment of accounts in 1999 §§ 9-404 through 9-406.   Perfection of assignments of accounts may be accomplished by filing under Article 9.

(4) *Miscellaneous Security Devices.* *Leases* of goods and *consignments* of goods are also sometimes in such form as to be secured transactions. In particular, the so-called *bailment lease* has been used as a security device closely resembling a conditional sale. Such security devices or others may also be secured transactions under Article 9. Another kind of security device is an *equipment trust* taken on such items as railway equipment, buses, airplanes and like items.

CHAPTER 2

THE SECURITY AGREEMENT

§ 1. Necessity of Agreement

A security interest cannot attach, and thus cannot be enforceable against the debtor with respect to the collateral, unless there is an agreement. Such an agreement is referred to as a *security agreement*. See 1999 §§ 9-203(b)(3), 9-102(a) (73). The term "security agreement" is defined as "an agreement which creates or provides for a security interest." 1999 § 9-102(a)(73).

Agreement is defined in pre-revision § 1-201(3) as "the bargain of the parties in fact as found in their language or by implication from other circumstances including course of dealing or usage of trade or course of performance.... Whether an agreement has legal consequences is determined by the provisions of [the Uniform Commercial Code], if applicable; otherwise by the law of contracts...." Similarly, see revised § 1-201(b)(3).

The agreement in a secured transaction is also a *contract*. The latter term is defined as "the total legal obligation which results from the parties' agreement as affected by [the Uniform Commercial Code] and any other applicable rules of law." Pre-revision § 1-201(11); revised § 1-201(b)(12).

Even where the secured party is in possession of the collateral, it must be kept in mind that an agreement is necessary, although it need not be in writing. Thus, a judgment creditor who seizes a debtor's property pursuant to attachment, garnishment or execution has no security interest under Article 9 of the Code. Rather, such a creditor has a judicial lien as provided by law outside the Code.

§ 2.   1999 Article 9 Security Agreement Requirements

a. Requirement of a Record

Although there are exceptions discussed below, 1999 Article 9 requires a *record* of the security agreement in order that the security interest attach, that is, be enforceable against the debtor with respect to the collateral. *Specifically*, the debtor must have authenticated a security agreement. See 1999 § 9-203(b)(3)(A). A *security agreement* means an agreement that creates or provides for a security interest. See 1999 § 9-102(a)(73).

A debtor can authenticate a security agreement in two ways. The debtor might *sign* a written security agreement. See 1999 § 9-102(a)(7)(a). *Signed* includes any symbol executed or adopted by a party with the present intention to authenticate a writing. See pre-revision § 1-201(39) and revised § 1-201(b)(37). A *writing* includes printing, typewriting or any other intentional reduction to tangible form. See pre-revision § 1-201(46) and revised § 1-201(b)(43).

The 1999 Article 9 also recognizes intangible security agreements providing that a debtor *authenticates* a security agreement by executing or otherwise adopting a symbol, or by encrypting or similarly processing a *record* in whole or in part, with the present intention of adopting a record. See 1999 § 9-102(a)(7)(b). A *record* means information that is inscribed on a tangible medium or which is stored in an electronic or other medium and is retrievable in perceivable form. See 1999 § 9-102(a)(69). Thus, the 1999 Code adjusts Article 9 to reflect current commercial practice that may include electronic security agreements. See Comment 9, 1999 § 9-102.

b. When Record Is Not Necessary

Under the 1999 Article 9, under some circumstances a *record* of a security agreement is not necessary. Where there is no such record, if the collateral is not a certificated security and is in the possession of a secured party pursuant to the debtor's security agreement, the security interest will still attach. See 1999 §§ 9-203(b) (3)(B), 9-313. When the secured party takes possession of the collateral, the secured transaction is commonly called a *pledge.*

Although a record of the security agreement is not legally necessary when the secured party is in possession, a record may nonetheless be desirable in order to set forth the various rights of the parties, the debt secured and like matters.

The requirement of a record of the security agreement is also dispensed with under the 1999 Article 9 in a few special situations which, though technically within Article 9, are not the ordinary type of secured transaction.

First, no record of a security agreement is necessary to create a security interest of a collecting bank under § 4-210. A collecting bank has a security interest in items and proceeds thereof held for collection under that Article 4 provision when it permits the withdrawal or application of credit given for an item, i.e., a deposited check, when it gives credit available for withdrawal as a matter of right, or when it makes an advance on or against an item.

Example. Bank B takes a check on deposit from its customer A, drawn by D on Bank C. B permits A to withdraw the amount of the check before collection is made (B permits A to draw against uncollected funds). B has a security interest in the check which may be enforced against the drawer D if the check is not paid by Bank C. No security agreement is necessary. Likewise, no filing is necessary.

Second, no record of a security agreement is necessary when a security interest arises under UCC Article 2 on Sales, or UCC Article 2A on Leases. Under 1999 § 9-110, a security interest arising solely under the Article on Sales or the Article on Leases is also subject to Article 9 on Secured Transactions. However, to the extent that and so long as *the debtor does not have or does not lawfully obtain possession of the goods*: (a) no security agreement is necessary; (b) no filing is required to perfect the security interest; and (c) the rights of the parties on default are governed by Articles 2 and 2A. The above rules apply only when the buyer has not received possession of the goods in a sales transaction; if the buyer receives possession of the goods, with the seller reserving title or a security interest for the price, Article 9 fully applies and a written security agreement is necessary.

Third, the 1999 Code does not require a record of the security agreement if the collateral is a certificated security in registered form and the security certificate has been delivered to the secured party pursuant to the debtor's security agreement. See 1999 §§ 9-203(b)(3)(C), 8-301. Generally, as to investment securities collateral, see Chapter 1, § 9a(3) and Chapter 4, § 4b.

Fourth, the 1999 Code does not require a record of the security agreement if the collateral is a deposit account, electronic chattel paper, investment property, or letter-of-credit rights, and the secured party has *control* of such property. See 1999 §§ 9-203(b)(3)(D), 9-104 through 9-107. *Control* under these 1999 Code sections essentially requires the secured party to have the collateral transferred to it or that the secured party otherwise have control over the collateral pursuant to an instruction contained in an authenticated record.

c. Formal Requirements of Record of Security Agreement Under 1999 Article 9.

(1) Debtor's Authentication

The 1999 Code requires the debtor to *authenticate* the security agreement. 1999 § 9-203(b)(3)(A). Recall from prior discussion that a security agreement is an agreement that creates or provides for a security interest. See 1999 § 9-102(a)(73). Authentication can occur in two ways. One method of authentication occurs when the debtor signs a written security agreement. See 1999 § 9-102(a)(7) (a). *Signed* includes any symbol executed or adopted by the party with the present intention to authenticate a writing. See pre-revision § 1-201(39) and revised § 1-201(b)(37). A second method of authentication occurs when the debtor executes or otherwise adopts a symbol, or encrypts or similarly processes a *record* in whole or in part, with the present intention of adopting the record. See 1999 § 9-102(a)(7)(B). A *record* is information that is inscribed on a tangible medium or which is stored in an electronic or other medium and is retrievable in perceivable form. See 1999 § 9-102 (a)(69).

There is no requirement of a *formal* or *complete* signature of the debtor, a signature need not be under seal, and agency concepts from the common law remain applicable where an agent signs or otherwise authenticates a security agreement on behalf of a principal. See pre-revision § 1-201(39), Comment 39 to pre-revision § 1-201, revised § 1-201(b)(37), Comment 37 to revised § 1-201, § 2-203, pre-revision § 1-103 and revised § 1-103(b). See for other discussion of signatures, Chapters 3 and 5.

(2) *Description of Collateral*

The record of the security agreement must contain a description of the collateral. See 1999 § 9-203 (b)(3)(A). There is no requirement that the description be specific or detailed. In this connection, 1999 § 9-108(a) states that "a description of personal... property is sufficient, whether or not it is specific, if it reasonably identifies what is described."

The 1999 Code provides examples of reasonable identification. See 1999 § 9-108(b). A description of collateral reasonably identifies the collateral if it identifies the collateral by specific listing, category, a type of collateral defined in the Code, quality, computational or allocational formula or procedure or any other method, if the identity of the collateral is objectively determinable. On the other hand, the 1999 Code as to the security agreement does not permit supergeneric descriptions such as "all the debtor's assets" or "all the debtor's personal property." See 1999 § 9-108(c).

Investment property is treated somewhat differently. Subject to one caveat, such collateral must be described as "investment property" or by the terms "security entitlement," "securities account," or "commodity account," where appropriate. The description also is sufficient if it describes the underlying financial asset or commodity account. See 1999 § 9-108(d).

The above-mentioned caveat is provided in 1999 § 9-108(e). As to collateral in the form of a security entitlement, a securities account or commodity account, and commercial tort claim, or in a consumer transaction, or as to consumer goods, a description only by the type of collateral defined in the UCC is insufficient. For example, "all existing and after-acquired investment property" without more would be an insufficient description. See 1999 § 9-108, Comment 5.

(3) *Description of Real Estate*

The 1999 Article 9 requires in one instance that the record of the security agreement describe real estate. Under 1999 § 9-203(b)(3)(A), description of the land concerned is necessary if the security interest is in timber to be cut. The description need not be the formal or technical style used generally when land is described in a real estate deed or mortgage. A description of real property is sufficient, whether or not it is specific, if it reasonably identifies what is described. See 1999 § 9-108(a).

§ 3. Grant of Security Interest

The security agreement must create or provide for a security interest. This accords with the definition of *security agreement* set forth in § 1 of this chapter. In other words, if the security agreement does not contain some language indicating that a security interest in described collateral is granted, the agreement is not a security agreement. However, Article 9 does not require particular language to evidence the grant of a security interest but, rather, is silent on the matter.

Example. Debtor signed a promissory note payable to Creditor for $150,000 which stated that it is secured by a security agreement between Debtor and T (a prior lender) and by a financing statement filed by T. The note further stated that it is secured by security interests in a security agreement to be delivered by Debtor to Creditor (a subsequent lender who paid off the $65,000 former loan to T and advanced an additional $85,000) which security agreement covers the collateral also covered in the prior security agreement. No new security agreement was entered into between Debtor and Creditor, but a financing statement in proper form and describing the same collateral covered in the earlier security agreement with T was properly filed. There was also "a group of letters" between Debtor and Creditor "constituting the course of dealing between the parties." The note, financing statement and correspondence, together, are sufficient to establish that the parties intended a security agreement to be created and are sufficient to create a security interest.

While it is necessary under the 1999 Code that a written security agreement be signed by the debtor or a record of security agreement be authenticated by the debtor, describe the collateral (and in one instance describe real estate) and perhaps have language that can be taken as evidencing an intent to grant a security interest, writings and other records purporting to evidence other kinds of transactions may nonetheless be considered as evidencing secured transactions. Such "disguised" secured transactions are discussed in § 5a of this chapter.

§ 4.   Necessity of Reference to Proceeds

Proceeds includes whatever is received by the debtor upon the sale, exchange, collection or other disposition of collateral or proceeds. See 1999 § 9-

102(a)(64). The secured party would like to have a security interest in such proceeds. The Code permits attachment of a security interest to traceable, that is identifiable, proceeds. See 1999 § 9-315(a)(2).

The 1999 Code takes the position that *no reference to proceeds is necessary in the security agreement.* See 1999 § 9-203(f) which states that "[t]he attachment of the security interest in collateral gives the secured party the right to proceeds ...."

This Code provision is based on the assumption that parties to a secured transaction intend to cover proceeds, unless otherwise agreed. There appears to be no purpose in requiring a specific reference to proceeds in a security agreement, and such a requirement would likely be a trap for a secured party who was careless in drafting a security agreement.

§ 5.   Agreement in Other Form as Security Agreement

a. *"Disguised" Security Agreements*

Although a security agreement must meet the basic requirements described in § 2 of this chapter, certain kinds of transactions covered by written agreements or other records of agreements and purportedly not labeled as secured transactions may nonetheless be so regarded. In other words, some transactions may be cast in other forms in writings or other records but still fall within the category of secured transactions and thus within the scope of UCC Article 9.

The transactions purportedly agreed upon may so closely resemble secured transactions as to be considered secured transactions, no matter how "disguised" in terminology. Examples such as sales reserving title in the seller, bills of sale, leases and consignments are discussed below.

b. *Reservation of Title in Seller*

It is declared in Article 2 of the Code governing Sales that any retention or reservation by the seller of title (property) in goods shipped or delivered to the buyer is limited in effect to a reservation of a security interest. See §§ 2-401(1) and 2-505. Similarly, as to leases see § 2A-508(5). In other words, a sale of goods in a transaction whereby title is expressly retained by the seller until the buyer pays the price is a secured transaction within the scope of Article 9, and the seller has a security interest in the goods for the payment of the price. Such a transaction under pre-Code law was often considered a conditional sale.

While the rule of § 2-401(1) described above applies when the buyer obtains delivery of the goods without paying the price, UCC Article 9 sets forth a different rule to govern instances where the buyer has not received possession of the goods. Under 1999 § 9-110, no security agreement is necessary nor is any filing required to perfect the security interest. Moreover, the rights of the parties on default are governed by Article 2 on Sales. In any other respect, Article 9 governs the transaction.

c. Bill of Sale

Article 2 of the Uniform Commercial Code on Sales applies to transactions in goods, but does not apply to any transaction which, although in the form of an unconditional contract to sell or present sale, is intended to operate only as a security transaction. See § 2-102. While under the 1999 Article 9 an authenticated record is usually required, and although a security agreement is defined in 1999 § 9-102(a)(73) as an agreement which creates or provides for a security interest, this does not reject the deeply rooted doctrine that a bill of sale, although absolute in form, may be shown to have been in fact given as security. Under Article 9, as under prior law, a debtor may show by parol evidence that a transfer purporting to be absolute was in fact one for security and may then, on payment of the debt, assert their fundamental right to return of the collateral and execution of an acknowledgment of satisfaction.

d. Lease of Personal Property

A secured transaction may arise under 1999 Article 9 where personal property is leased and the lease is intended as security.   See 1999 § 9-109(a)(1). Some difficulty has arisen in cases where a lease is regarded as a secured transaction and where the lessor (secured party) failed to file under Article 9 and thus had an unperfected security interest. Leases of personal property often closely resemble installment purchases of goods with retention of title in the seller-"lessor" until payment is made in full.

In this connection, the definition of security interest in pre-revision § 1-201(37) states in part:

"... Whether a transaction creates a lease or security interest is determined by the facts of each case; however, a transaction creates a security interest if the consideration the lessee is to pay the lessor for the right to possession and use of the goods is an *obligation for the term of the lease not subject to termination by the lessee....*" [Emphasis added.]

Similarly, see revised § 1-203(a), (b).

In addition to an obligation for the term of the lease, one of four other criterions must be satisfied for the "lease" to be considered a security agreement:

(1) The original term of the lease must be equal to or greater than the remaining economic life of the goods; or

(2) The lessee is bound to renew the lease for the remaining economic life of the goods or is bound to become the owner of the goods; or

(3) The lessee must have an option to renew the lease for the remaining economic life of the goods for no additional consideration upon compliance with the lease agreement; or

(4) The lessee must have an option to become the owner of the goods for no additional consideration or nominal consideration upon compliance with the lease agreement.

The Code also sets forth factors of a lease agreement that do not indicate the agreement creates a security interest. See, in that regard, pre-revision § 1-201(37) and revised § 1-203(c).

Example 1. Equipment was leased by B to A at a monthly rate with A having an option at the end of the lease period to purchase the equipment and have 85 percent of the rental payments applied toward such purchase. Such a lease is a secured transaction where the lessee is obligated to pay the lessor for the term of the lease and has no right of termination. See pre-revision § 1-201(37) and revised § 1-203.

Example 2. Equipment was leased from B to A at a monthly rate with A having an option at the end of the lease period to purchase the equipment and have 75 percent of the rental payments applied toward such purchase up to but not exceeding 75 percent of the price. Such a lease is *not* a secured transaction even if the lessee could not terminate the lease, because the lessee still must pay more than a *nominal amount* to purchase the equipment at the end of the lease period. See pre-revision § 1-201(37) and revised § 1-203.

e. Consignment of Personal Property

A consignment might be described as an entrustment or bailment of goods by one person (consignor) to another person (consignee) under an arrangement whereby the consignee is to sell the goods for the consignor and remit the sales proceeds to the consignor. If the consignee is unable to sell the goods, they may return them to the consignor. In the Sales Article of the Code, such a consignment is considered a *sale or return*. See § 2-326(1)(b).

1999 Article 9 flatly states that the Article applies to consignments. See 1999 § 9-109(a)(4). The 1999 Article § 9-102(a)(20) defines "consignment" as a transaction, regardless of its form, in which a person delivers goods to a merchant for the purpose of sale. The merchant must deal in goods of this kind under a name other than the name of the person making delivery and must not be an auctioneer and the merchant must not generally be known by its creditors to be substantially engaged in selling goods of others. See 1999 § 9-102(a)(20)(A). The aggregate value of the goods must be $1,000 or more at the time of delivery. See 1999 § 9-102(a) (20)(B). The goods must not be consumer goods immediately before delivery [1999 § 9-102(a)(20) (C)] and the transaction must not create a security interest that secures an obligation [1999 § 9-102(a) (20)(D)].

Thus, under 1999 Article 9 some "true" consignments as described above, that is a bailment of goods for the purpose of sale by the bailee, are within the scope of UCC Article 9. In most consignment transactions, the consignor will file a financing statement in order to protect its interest against creditors of the consignee. Additionally, a true consignment under the 1999 Article 9 is subject to all of Article 9, except where otherwise stated, because the true consignment is within the scope of the 1999 Article 9. Thus, the rules pertaining to lien creditors, buyers, attachment and perfection, and the priority of competing security interests apply to consigned goods. The 1999 Article does provide that the relationship of the consignor and consignee is left to other law and that the consignor has no duties under Part 6 of the 1999 Article 9 that pertains to default and enforcement of security interests. See 1999 § 9-109, Comment 6.

§ 6. Other Terms in Security Agreement

a. Freedom of Contract

A security agreement may, and usually does, contain a number of "optional" provisions in addition to those required under 1999 § 9-203(b)(3)(A).

The Uniform Commercial Code permits broad freedom of contract with respect to provisions which may be incorporated in a security agreement. Under the 1999 Article 9, § 9-201 declares that, except as otherwise provided by the Code, "a security agreement is effective according to its terms between the parties, against purchasers of the collateral and against creditors." Note also that the last paragraph of the Comment to 1972 § 9-101 stated that the rules set out in Article 9 are principally concerned with the limits of the secured party's protection against purchasers from and creditors of the debtor. It then stated: "Except for the procedure on default, freedom of contract prevails between the immediate parties to the secured transaction." The 1999 Article 9 continues to honor this freedom of contract approach.

A consonant provision applicable to the Code generally, pre-revision § 1-102(3), permits variation of Code provisions by agreement, except as otherwise provided in the Code, and then states that "the obligations of good faith, diligence, reasonableness and care" prescribed by the Code may not be disclaimed by agreement. However, the parties "may by agreement determine the standards by which the performance of such obligations is to be measured if such standards are not manifestly unreasonable." Similarly, see revised § 1-302.

In addition to the general requirements of good faith, diligence, reasonableness and care, referred to above, some other Article 9 provisions as they may affect third persons may not be varied by agreement between the debtor and the secured party. These include provisions as to priorities between the secured party and a third person, such as purchasers of the collateral, other creditors of the debtor and other secured parties (1999 §§ 9-315, 9-317, 9-320, 9-322 through 9-324, 9-330 through 9-331, 9-333 through 9-336).

Moreover, the freedom of contract permitted under Article 9 may be limited by regulatory statutes outside the Code governing such matters as usury, small loans, retail installment sales or the like. Other consumer-protection statutes such as the Uniform Consumer Credit Code also fall within that category. See 1999 § 9-201.

Some other provisions which are ineffective if included in a security agreement include:

(1) A term prohibiting transfer of the debtor's equity in the collateral, 1999 § 9-401(b). See Chapter 3, § 9.

(2) A term waiving priority rules of Article 9, unless assented to by affected third persons, Comment 2 to 1999 § 9-201.

(3) A term waiving or varying certain rights and duties upon default, 1999 § 9-602.

(4) An "unconscionable" term in a contract for the sale of goods, § 2-302. This latter restriction applies in a sale of goods on credit creating a secu-

rity interest in the goods, but it is not so clear as to the extent that "unconscionability" affects a secured transaction arising under other circumstances.

Some other limitations on freedom of contract are discussed in this chapter in connection with after-acquired property provisions in security agreements and provisions permitting the secured party to accelerate payment or to require additional collateral.

b. *After-Acquired Property as Collateral*

(1) *Generally May be Covered*

With exceptions discussed below relating to consumer goods, "a security agreement may create or provide for a security interest in after-acquired collateral." 1999 § 9-204(a).

Examples of after-acquired property clauses which are effective include clauses such as "all inventory now or hereafter acquired by Debtor"; "all accounts due or to become due to Debtor"; or "all contents of Debtor's restaurant together with all property and articles now, and which may hereafter be used or mixed with, added to or attached to or substituted for, any of the foregoing property."

Yet another example is the following: The security interest of the secured party under this agreement extends to all collateral of the kind which is the subject of this agreement which the debtor may acquire at any time during the continuation of this agreement in connection with the operation of the business of the debtor.

The coverage of after-acquired property permitted under the Code accepts the principle of a "continuing general lien" and rejects the judicial attitude of former law against after-acquired property clauses. The widespread nineteenth century prejudice against the "floating charge" was based on a feeling, often inarticulate in the opinions, that a commercial borrower should not be allowed to encumber all their assets present and future, and that, for the protection not only of the borrower but of their other creditors, a cushion of free assets should be preserved. Article 9 rejects that view on the ground that it was not effective under pre-Code law. A number of pre-Code devices such as field warehousing, trust receipts and factor's liens could be used to avoid the former rule against encumbrance of all of the debtor's assets. See Comment 2 to 1999 § 9-204.

After-acquired property that may be embraced in a security agreement may include the *increase* of existing collateral.

Example. A security agreement covering all cattle of the debtor also covers the increase where one of the group of cattle covered gives birth to a calf.

Moreover, after-acquired property may include the *products* of collateral.

Example. Raw materials which are covered in a security agreement are converted into a finished product, which is also covered.

Notwithstanding that a security interest may be taken in after-acquired property, this does not mean that the interest is proof against subordination or defeat. In this connection, 1999 § 9-324 should be consulted on when such a security interest may be subordinated to a conflicting purchase-money security interest of another person in the same collateral.

(2) *Limitation as to Consumer Goods*

"A security interest does not attach under a term constituting an after-acquired property clause...to consumer goods, other than an accession, unless the debtor acquires rights in them within 10 days after the secured party gives value...." 1999 § 9-204(b)(1). The 1999 Code also does not permit attachment of a security interest by way of an after-acquired property clause to a commercial tort claim. See

1999 § 9-204(b)(2).

This limitation departs from the general policy of permitting security interests to cover after-acquired property in order to protect a necessitous consumer from encumbering all their present and future assets. However, consumer goods acquired within 10 days after the secured party gives value may be covered.

Accessions may also be covered. For example, if a security interest is taken in an automobile and a new engine is installed, the security interest may cover the engine.

c. Future Advances

"A security agreement may provide that collateral secures...future advances or other value, whether or not the advances or value are given pursuant to commitment." 1999 § 9-204(c). "Pursuant to commitment" means "pursuant to the secured party's obligation, whether or not a subsequent event of default or other event not within the secured parties' control has relieved or may relieve the secured party from its obligation." 1999 § 9-102(a)(68).

Example of "future advance" clause: The security interest herein created shall also secure all other indebtedness, obligations and liabilities of the debtor to the secured party, now existing and hereafter arising, including future advances, howsoever evidenced or created, actual, direct, contingent or otherwise.

At common law and under chattel mortgage statutes there was a vaguely articulated prejudice against future advance agreements comparable to the prejudice against after-acquired property interests. In line with the policy of Article 9 permitting after-acquired property interests, future advances are also validated, provided only that the obligation be covered in the security agreement. See Comment 5 to 1999 § 9-204. However, if the security agreement fails to provide for future advances, the security interest taken in the collateral arguably will cover only the original debt and not future advances made.

Example. Debtor borrowed $25,000 on a promissory note. A security agreement was also signed describing the collateral as "all widgets in Debtor's possession." The security agreement also stated that the collateral "secures payment of the debt evidenced by the note of the same date and also any and all liabilities of Debtor to Creditor under this agreement or said note or any renewal or extension thereof." Debtor later borrowed an additional $25,000 and gave another note for that sum. The collateral covered in the security agreement does not secure the additional borrowing, since the security agreement provided only for renewals or extensions of the original debt and not for additional indebtedness.

On the other hand, where a priority dispute arises involving UCC Article 9 claimants, some courts have held that even though a security agreement does not expressly include a future advance clause, a later advance will be secured by the security interest created by the security agreement. Other courts, in the case of a priority dispute involving UCC Article 9 claimants have held to the contrary and required an express future advance clause to be included in the security agreement for a later advance to be effectively secured by the security interest created in that security agreement.

Recognition of the validity of the security interest on after-acquired property and the security interest for future advances facilitates the financing of *inventory* and *accounts* (accounts receivable) where the collateral turns over, e.g., a security interest on a shifting stock of goods. The secured party thus may make present and future advances to the debtor (often referred to as revolving credits) secured by both present and after-acquired inventory or accounts or both. This results in what is often called a *floating lien*. See Comment 2 to 1999 § 9-204.

d. Option to Accelerate Payment or Require Additional Collateral

Frequently, a security agreement calling for payments at fixed times will have a provision for acceleration of payment. Acceleration may be specified at the secured party's option upon the happening of certain events, such as nonpayment of principal or interest on the debt, nonperformance by the debtor of duties required in the security agreement, bankruptcy or insolvency on the part of the debtor, or even events beyond the debtor's control, such as the debtor's death (or the death of the key individual in the debtor's organization). Such provisions are generally given effect.

Another type of acceleration provision permits the secured party to accelerate payment "at will" or "when they deem themselves insecure" or in words of similar import. The right of the secured party to accelerate at their option under such a provision is limited in pre-revision § 1-208 and revised § 1-309; the secured party may act only "if that party in good faith believes that the prospect of payment or performance is impaired." However, the burden of establishing lack of good faith is on the party against whom the power has been exercised.

In other words, under such a provision, the secured party may not accelerate payment at whim or for some reason not related to the prospect of payment by the debtor, but the debtor must prove that any acceleration made was capricious and not related to the prospect of payment.

Another kind of provision sometimes found in security agreements permits the secured party to require the debtor to put up additional collateral upon the happening of certain events, such as impairment of the market value of the existing collateral. Sometimes, a provision as to additional collateral merely permits the secured party to require such "at will" or "when they deem themselves insecure" or in words of similar import. Pre-revision § 1-208 and revised § 1-309 restrict this right to require additional collateral at will only if the secured party "in good faith believes that the prospect of payment or performance is impaired." However, the burden of establishing lack of good faith is on the party against whom the power has been exercised.

§ 7. Additional "Optional" Terms

Some additional provisions (discussed elsewhere in this chapter and in Chapter 3, § 3) which may be included in a security agreement include: (1) giving the debtor liberty to use or dispose of the collateral or to make their own collections of accounts of chattel paper; (2) waiver by the debtor of defenses when the security interest is assigned; (3) subordination of the security interest in favor of the interest of a third person; (4) permitting future advances or covering after-acquired property; (5) permitting acceleration or requiring additional collateral; or (6) giving or limiting sales warranties.

Some other optional terms may also be included which are not specifically dealt with in Article 9. Such terms may include the following:

a. The amount of debt and the terms of payment.

Unlike some pre-Code chattel mortgage statutes, the security agreement does not have to set forth the debt or related matters. However, it is obvious that there must be a debt or obligation, and the security agreement or some other writing (such as a promissory note) generally sets forth provisions respecting the debt. This may include principal, interest or finance charges (subject to limitations in usury or consumer credit statutes outside the Code), other charges permitted by law, provision for attorneys' fees and costs of collection where permitted by law, provision for confession of judgment where permitted by law, and some statement of the terms of repayment, maturity and like matters.

b. Duties of the debtor respecting the collateral.

These may include duties relating to care or maintenance of the collateral, keeping it at a designated place, using it only in a certain manner, or payment of taxes, insurance premiums and other expenses connected with the collateral.

c. Other duties or restrictions on the debtor.

These may include the furnishing of financial statements or reports to the secured party, restrictions on the payment of dividends or other distribution of profits, restrictions on the incurring of other indebtedness or the subjecting of the collateral to other liens or security interests.

d. Duties as to proceeds.

The security agreement may require the debtor to turn over proceeds from the sale of collateral periodically to the secured party, to execute written assignments of accounts and similar matters.

e. Events of default.

A security agreement generally sets forth various acts or occurrences that may constitute events of default. The most common event of default is nonpayment of principal or interest or nonpayment of an installment when due. Other events may consist of failure on the part of the debtor to comply with other duties or requirements set forth in the security agreement, unauthorized sale or removal of the collateral, bankruptcy or insolvency of the debtor, failure of the debtor to pay debts to third persons when due and many other possible acts or occurrences. Upon the happening of one or more events of default, the secured party is generally given the option of accelerating payment and may resort to the "default" provisions of Article 9 (1999 §§ 9-601 through 9-628). However, the secured party may not take "default" action in the absence of an event of default set forth in the security agreement. See Chapter 9, § 1.

§ 8. Subordination Agreements

Sometimes a security interest may be subordinated by agreement to another security interest or to a claim of some other person. Nothing in Article 9 prevents subordination by agreement by any person entitled to priority. 1999 § 9-339. However, the agreement must be made by the person willing to subordinate their interest; their rights cannot be adversely affected by an agreement to which they are not a party. See Comment 2 to 1999 § 9-339.

A related provision of Article 1, drafted as an "optional provision" and not enacted in all Code jurisdictions, permits subordination of one obligation to payment of another obligation by agreement of the subordinating person with either the obligor or the beneficiary of the other obligation. However, such a subordination does not itself create a security interest as against either the common debtor or a subordinated creditor, and the provision is declared as stating the existing law (common law) and not changing it. Pre-revision § 1-209 and revised § 1-310.

There is nothing in the above provision to prevent an agreement in which a creditor subordinates their interest to another creditor and also gives a security interest in his right to payment from the debtor to such other creditor.

CHAPTER 3

RELATIONSHIP OF THE
PARTIES PRIOR TO DEFAULT

§ 1.   Attachment of Security Interest

Attachment of a security interest might be considered as equivalent to creation of a security interest. In other words, unless there is attachment of a security interest, there is no security interest whatever. But once a security interest has attached, the secured party has the right to enforce the security interest and realize on the collateral, at least against the debtor.

Additionally, attachment of a security interest is necessary in order that the security interest can be perfected, thereby making it to the extent possible effective against third parties, including a bankruptcy trustee. Perfection of security interests is discussed in Chapters 4, 5 and 6.

The 1999 Code provides that for a security interest to attach to collateral three requirements must be met. See 1999 § 9-203(b). The three requirements are as follows:

First, *value* must be given. This requirement is discussed in § 1a of this chapter which follows.

Second, the debtor must have *rights* in the collateral. This requirement is discussed in § 1b of this chapter which also follows.

Third, there must be an *agreement*. The debtor usually must have authenticated a security agreement. 1999 § 9-203(b)(3)(A). This requirement of an authenticated security agreement is discussed at Chapter 2, § 2a. There are situations in which an authenticated security agreement is not necessary. 1999 § 9-203(b)(3)(B), (C) and (D). All of these situations are discussed at Chapter 2, § 2b.

The 1999 Code provides that a security interest attaches to collateral when it becomes enforceable against the debtor with respect to the collateral. This is the case unless an agreement expressly postpones the time of attachment. 1999 § 9-203(a).

a. Requirement of Value

A security interest cannot attach under the 1999 Code unless value is given.   1999 § 9-203(b)(1). The term "value" is defined in pre-revision § 1-201(44) and revised § 1-204 and has not been redefined by the 1999 Code within Article 9.

According to that definition, a person gives value for rights if they acquire them:

"(1) in return for a binding commitment to extend credit or for the extension of immediately available credit whether or not drawn upon and whether or not a charge-back is provided for in the event of difficulties in collection; or

(2) as security for or in total or partial satisfaction of a pre-existing claim; or

(3) by accepting delivery pursuant to a pre-existing contract for purchase; or

(4) generally, in return for any consideration sufficient to support a simple contract."

From the above definition, it can be seen that *value* is not only *consideration* in the ordinary sense under the law of contracts, but is also the taking of security for an *antecedent debt*. In this regard, the concept of value goes beyond the ordinary rules of the law of contracts which generally reject the enforceability of a promise based on past consideration.

Example 1. Debtor purchased goods from Creditor on open account. When Debtor is unable to pay, they enter into a security agreement granting Creditor a security interest in the goods. Value is given, even though the security interest is for an antecedent debt. The same is true if Debtor gives Creditor a security interest in goods other than those sold by Creditor.

Consideration in the ordinary sense used in the law of contracts is also value.

Example 2. Pursuant to a security agreement or conditional sales agreement, Seller sells or agrees to sell goods to Buyer on credit and reserves a security interest in the goods to secure the balance of the price. Value is given when Seller sells or agrees to sell the goods.

Example 3. Debtor bought goods from Seller on open account. When Debtor is unable to pay, they enter into a security agreement with Lender granting Lender a security interest in the goods. Lender assumes Debtor's debt to Seller. Value is given.

In connection with the definition of value as including a binding commitment to extend credit or the extension of credit, difficulty has sometimes arisen in determining in particular fact situations whether value was given at the time the secured party indicated its willingness to extend credit or at the later time that credit was extended.

Example 4. Debtor, desiring to purchase widgets from Seller, requested a loan of the purchase price

from Lender, and Debtor signed a security agreement granting Lender a security interest in the
widgets for any loan that Lender might make for the
purchase price. Seller delivered the widgets to
Debtor and billed Debtor for the price. Debtor
forwarded the bill to Lender and the latter paid
Seller. Value was not given until Lender paid the
bill, since there was no earlier commitment to
extend credit.

Example 5. The same facts exist as in Example
4 above, except that the security agreement provided
that Lender promised to make the loan if Debtor
purchased the widgets. Value was given at the time
the security agreement was entered into, since there
was a commitment to extend credit at that time.

b. Requirement That Debtor Have Rights in the Collateral

A security interest cannot attach under the 1999
Code unless the debtor has rights in the collateral.
Specifically, the 1999 Code provides that the debtor
must have rights in the collateral or the power to
transfer rights in the collateral to a secured party.
1999 § 9-203(b)(2).

The term "rights" is not defined [except that pre-
revision § 1-201(36) and revised § 1-201(b)(34)

declare that "rights" includes remedies]. Undoubt-edly, the debtor who owns the collateral has *rights* in it. Presumably, the debtor also has rights in the collateral when it is delivered to them or when they are in possession, whether or not they have legal title or ownership, at least in most instances. In certain other instances, the debtor not in possession may also have rights in the collateral.

Example 1. Buyer enters into an agreement with Lender to finance purchase of an automobile and gives Lender a security interest in the automobile. Buyer then goes to Dealer and enters into a binding written contract for sale of a specific automobile then in Dealer's showroom. Buyer has rights in the automobile at the time they enter into the contract for sale even though they have not obtained delivery. The reason is that Buyer has a special property and insurable interest in the automobile under § 2-501(1) in the Article on Sales. If Buyer had merely entered into a contract with Dealer to buy a particular kind and model of automobile at a stated price, but no specific car had been identified in the contract, Buyer would have no rights in any particular car meeting the description of the contract for sale.

Example 2. Financer repossessed an automobile and delivered it to Dealer for repairs. Dealer had entered into a security agreement with Second

Financer covering all of Dealer's inventory. Second Financer has no security interest in the automobile since Dealer has no rights in that particular car.

Official Comment 6 to 1999 § 9-203 elaborates on this "rights" requirement. The 1999 Official Comment indicates that a debtor's limited rights in collateral, short of full ownership, are sufficient for a security interest to attach. However, the Comment mentions a "baseline" rule that a security interest attaches only to whatever rights a debtor may have. The Comment notes that there are exceptions to the baseline rule that enable a debtor to transfer, and a security interest to attach to, greater rights than the debtor has. Thus, 1999 § 9-203(b)(2) adds the phrase "or the power to transfer rights in the collateral to a secured party." These exceptions to the baseline rule are embodied in the priority rules of 1999 Code found in §§ 9-317—9-339 (1999).

Example. The owner of some pottery gives possession of the pottery to an art gallery and authorizes the gallery to sell the pottery for the owner, the gallery to receive a commission upon making a sale. If the art gallery cannot sell the pottery within six months, the pottery must be returned to the owner. This transaction is a "consignment." Assume that Big Bank has previously made a loan to the gallery and the gallery granted

Big Bank a security interest in all of its inventory of art presently owned and after acquired. Under the Code, the consigned pottery is subject to the claims of the gallery's creditors. In other words, Big Bank's security interest will attach to the consigned pottery because the debtor-gallery has the power to transfer rights to the secured party. If the security interest has priority over the owner-consignor's interest under an applicable priority rule, Big Bank will be able to enforce the security interest in the consigned pottery even though the gallery held only a consignee's interest in the pottery. For example, if the owner of the pottery does not file a financing statement and does not give notice to Big Bank, Big Bank has priority over the owner-consignor's interest. See 1999 §§ 9-316, 9-324(b) and § 2-236(3)(c). For other discussions of consignments, see Chapter 2, § 5e.

§ 2. Title to the Collateral

Article 9 of the Code does not determine whether *title* to the collateral is in the debtor or in the secured party and adopts neither a "title theory" nor a "lien theory" of security interests. Pre-Code chattel mortgage laws of some states adopted a "title theory" whereby title was in the mortgagor while the mortgagee had a lien on the property.

Instead, Article 9 declares in 1999 § 9-202 that rights, obligations and remedies under Article 9 do not depend on the location of title in the debtor or in the secured party. In other words, *title is largely irrelevant in a secured transaction under Article 9.*

The location of title may be relevant under other law for certain other purposes outside the scope of Article 9, as for example determining the owner of goods under a tax law. Where title is relevant, the use of a form traditionally regarded as determinative of title might be considered as evidencing the intention of the parties. Moreover, where a secured transaction arises in connection with a sale of goods, the location of title to the extent that it is relevant may be determined by resorting to § 2-401.

§ 3. Right of Debtor to Use or Dispose of Collateral

It is a matter for agreement between the debtor and secured party whether the debtor is to have possession of the collateral. It is also a matter for agreement whether the debtor has the right to sell the collateral, to receive and handle the proceeds of sale or to collect accounts of those to whom the debtor makes sales.

The 1999 Code at § 9-205 provides that a security

interest is "not invalid as fraudulent against creditors solely because" the debtor can use, commingle or dispose of collateral; collect or otherwise deal with collateral; accept returns or make repossessions of collateral; or use proceeds of collateral. But this does not "relax the requirements of possession if attachment, perfection, or enforcement of a security interest depends upon possession of the collateral by the secured party."

In other words, pre-Code holdings of a number of jurisdictions which invalidated security interests where the debtor was permitted freely to sell the collateral, collect the proceeds of sale and collect assigned accounts receivable are overturned by the Code. Comment 2 to 1999 § 9-205 expressly declares that the Code repeals the rule of Benedict v. Ratner, 268 U.S. 353 (1925), and similar cases which held such arrangements void because the debtor was given unfettered dominion or control over the collateral. The Benedict v. Ratner rule was sometimes thought to require lenders to observe a number of needless and costly formalities. For example, the debtor had to make daily remittances to the lender of all collections received, even though the account remitted was immediately returned to the debtor in order to keep the loan at an agreed level. See Comment 2 to 1999 § 9-205.

1999 §§ 9-204 and 9-205 thus have the effect of validating a floating charge or lien on shifting stock. It is a matter of agreement between the debtor and secured party as to the amount of policing or control the latter may exercise over the debtor's business operations or the control of the debtor's collateral. The Code provisions also permit both "notification" and "non-notification" financing secured by accounts. In other words, the agreement may permit debtors to collect their own accounts from account debtors without the necessity of giving notice to the account debtors that the accounts have been assigned. The agreement may also permit the secured party to notify the account debtors of the assignment and directly collect the accounts from such account debtors. See Comment 2 to 1999 § 9-205.

§ 4.   Rights and Duties When Secured Party Has Possession

Some common-law principles of law as to rights and duties of the respective parties when there is a pledge are codified in 1999 § 9-207, which applies to a pledge. Such principles are summarized as follows:

a. The pledgee (secured party in possession) must use reasonable care in the custody and preservation of the collateral.

Where the collateral is an instrument or chattel paper, reasonable care includes taking necessary steps to preserve rights against prior parties unless otherwise agreed.

Example 1. Debtor A pledged some stock of X Corporation owned by A with B to secure a loan from B to A. While B was in possession, X issued some rights to existing stockholders to purchase additional shares of X stock, which rights would expire if not exercised by a stated date. B, knowing of the existence of such rights, failed to notify A of their existence before the expiration date. B is liable to A for any loss sustained by A caused by B's failure, and B would be considered to have failed to exercise due care under § 9-207.

Example 2. Debtor F placed some stock of Y Corporation owned by F with G to secure a loan from G to F. While G was in possession, the stock declined greatly in value but G failed to sell. G as pledgee is not responsible for the decline in market value, particularly since F had equal opportunity with G to stay apprized of the declining value of the stock.

b. Expenses incurred in connection with the collateral are chargeable to the debtor and are also secured by the collateral.

c. The risk of accidental loss or damage is on the debtor to the extent of any deficiency in insurance coverage.

d. Any increase of the collateral, such as a stock dividend paid on pledged stock, becomes additional security for the debt. Any money received from the collateral, such as a cash dividend on pledged stock, may be remitted to the debtor but if not must be applied to the debt.

e. The collateral must be kept identifiable, but fungible collateral may be commingled. In other words, if collateral such as stock is pledged, it must be kept identifiable as the property of the particular debtor. But fungible collateral [see definition of *fungible* in pre-revision § 1-201(17) and revised § 1-201(b)(18)] such as pledged grain may be commingled with other similar collateral, such as a quantity of grain in a warehouse.

f. The pledgee may re-pledge the collateral upon terms which do not impair the debtor's right to redeem it. In other words, a pledgee or secured party may use the pledged collateral as security for their own debt and re-pledge it to a second pledgee. Although 1999 § 9-207 is silent regarding the debtor's right of redemption, that right remains. See Comment 5 to 1999 § 9-207. Also, the first pledgee faces possible liability if they re-pledge to a second pledgee who is known to be irresponsible.

g. A pledgee is liable for any loss caused by failure to exercise due care or any other failure described above, but does not lose their security interest. The rule is implied in 1999 § 9-207(a) on the pledgee's general duty of care. See also 1999 § 9-625(b).

h. Under limited circumstances, the pledgee may use or operate the collateral. This may be done to preserve it, or pursuant to court order, or (except with respect to consumer goods) as permitted in the security agreement.

§ 5. Rights When Secured Party Knows That Third Person Owns the Collateral

It is clear under the Code that a third person may sometimes put up for the debtor the collateral which is security for the debt, and such a third person falls within the definition of "debtor" in 1999 § 9-102(a)(28), even though not personally liable for the debt.

As a "debtor," such third persons have the rights of a "debtor" *when the secured party knows that the collateral is owned by the third person*, under 1999 § 9-605. The 1999 definition of "debtor" makes it clear that provisions of Article 9 apply to one who has an interest in the collateral even though not personally liable for the debt. See Comment 2(a), 1999 § 9-102. In short, under the 1999 Code such third persons enjoy the same rights of a "debtor" automatically.

Those rights of the third person include the right to receive from the secured party any surplus arising from collections made from account debtors or obligors and any surplus resulting from sale of the collateral. In addition, the third person *is not liable for any deficiency* following sale of the collateral, unless otherwise agreed.

Additional rights of such a third person include the following:

(1) to receive from the secured party statements of account of the indebtedness and of the collateral; and to recover any losses for failure of the secured party to furnish such;

(2) to receive notice of and to object to a secured party's proposal to retain the collateral in satisfaction of the indebtedness;

(3) to redeem the collateral;

(4) to obtain injunctive or other relief if the secured party is not proceeding in accordance with the provisions of the Code governing rights after default.

It should be repeated that the above rules apply only if the secured party knows that the collateral belongs to a third person. Short of such knowledge, the secured party may deal exclusively with the debtor who owes the obligation. Nor is the secured party under any duty of inquiry, and the Code does not deal with the matter of the authority of a debtor to put up property owned by someone else. See 1999 § 9-605.

§ 6.   Right of Debtor to Statement of Account or List of Collateral

A procedure is set forth in 1999 § 9-210 whereby a debtor may obtain from a secured party a statement of the amount due on the obligation and a statement of the collateral. Under 1999 § 9-210, the debtor can submit an authenticated record and request thereby a list of the collateral, a statement of account, or an accounting. The secured party has 14 days after receipt in which to respond. If the secured party fails to comply with the request for information, the secured party is liable to the debtor for $500 and for any damages caused by its failure. 1999 § 9-625(f). Additionally, to the extent a party is misled by the secured party's failure to respond to a request for a list of collateral, the secured party may claim an interest only as shown on the debtor's list. 1999 § 9-625(g).

The financing statement filed may disclose only that a secured party may have a security interest in specified types of collateral. Third parties are normally told neither the amount of the obligation secured nor which particular assets are covered. Since subsequent creditors and purchasers may legitimately need more detailed information, it is necessary to provide a procedure under which the secured party will be required to make disclosure.

On the other hand, the secured party should not be required to disclose details to any casual inquirer or competitor who asks for them. Thus, the right to demand disclosure is given only to the debtor, who will typically request a statement in connection with negotiations with subsequent creditors and purchasers or for the purpose of establishing their credit standing and proving which of their assets are free of the security interest.

§ 7. Modification or Exclusion of Sales Warranties

When a seller retains a purchase-money security interest in goods, Article 2 on Sales should govern the sale and any disclaimer, limitation or modification of the seller's warranties. Although the 1999 Code has no provision on point, the comments make it clear that Article 2 of the Code governs any disclaimer, limitation, or modification of the seller's warranties. See Comment 4 to 1999 § 9-403.

In other words, if a seller of goods on credit takes a purchase-money security interest in the goods, the Sales Article of the Code governs the existence of warranties concerning the quality of the goods and also governs the effectiveness of any attempt in the security agreement to exclude or limit such sales warranties. Warranties arising in connection with sales of goods may be express (§ 2-313) or implied (§§ 2-314 and 2-315), and a warranty of title is also generally given (§ 2-312). The effectiveness of language in a written sales agreement to exclude express or implied warranties is limited; such exclusions must meet certain standards (§ 2-316).

By making the Sales Article applicable, Article 9 has the effect of preventing a buyer from inadvertently abandoning their warranties by a "no warranties" term in the security agreement, when warranties have already been created under the sales agreement. Where the sales transaction and the purchase-money security transaction are evidenced by only one writing, that writing may disclaim, limit or modify warranties but only to the extent permitted by Article 2. See Comment 4 to 1999 § 9-403.

Example.   In connection with the sale of a quantity of widgets, a written sales contract expressly warranted the "marketability" of the goods. A separate written security agreement granting a purchase-money security interest in the widgets to the seller for the price contained a statement whereby the buyer acknowledged delivery of the goods purchased "without warranty, guarantee or representation of any kind or nature." The attempted exclusion in the security agreement is ineffective, since

Article 2 governs the sales warranties and attempts to disclaim them. Thus, in an action by the seller to enforce payment under the security agreement, the buyer may defend on the basis that the widgets were not marketable and the sales warranty was breached.

§ 8.   Secured Party Not Obligated on Debtor's Contract

The mere existence of a security interest or authority given to the debtor to dispose of or use collateral does not impose contract or tort liability upon the secured party for the debtor's acts or omissions. 1999 § 9-402.

The Comments to 1999 § 9-402 state that there were a few common-law decisions which suggested, if they did not hold, that a secured party who gave his debtor liberty of sale might be liable, as for example for breach of warranty, on the debtor's contracts of sale. This theory was grounded on the law of agency, the debtor being regarded as selling agent for the secured party as principal. 1999 § 9-402 rejects that theory.

The rights of a secured party as assignee are subject to defenses the account debtor has against the assignor and may be subject to setoff for claims of an account debtor against the assignor under 1999

§ 9-404(a). In addition,1999 § 9-404(b) and Comment 3 make it clear that the account debtor may not go further and assert affirmative rights of recovery from the assignee over and above any amounts assigned, for a default on the part of the assignor.

Example. Buyer bought a machine from Seller on credit. Seller assigned their right to the unpaid price to Financer. Because of a defect in the machine, Buyer sustained personal injuries. While Buyer (unless Buyer has validly waived their defenses against an assignee) may set off their claim against the assigned payments due on the machine, Buyer may not recover damages, over and above the payments due, from Financer on a theory of breach of warranty or other "products liability" theory of recovery.

§ 9. Transferability of Debtor's Rights in the Collateral

The debtor's rights in collateral may be *voluntarily* or *involuntarily* transferred (by way of sale, creation of a security interest, attachment, levy, garnishment or other judicial process) notwithstanding a provision in the security agreement prohibiting any transfer or making the transfer constitute an event of default. 1999 § 9-401.

In other words, the debtor can always voluntarily transfer their equity in the collateral subject to the security interest. Their equity may also be reached by third persons, such as other creditors, but subject to the security interest if perfected. The security agreement may not prohibit such a transfer, but it can make the transfer an event of default. However, even in the latter case, the transferee takes subject to the security interest.

Where a security interest is in inventory, difficult problems arise with reference to attachment and levy. If a debt of $100,000 is secured by inventory worth $200,000, the debtor's equity may be reached. But if by attachment and levy certain units of the inventory are seized, the determination of the debtor's equity in the units seized is not a simple matter. The solution to this problem is left to the courts, but procedures such as marshaling of assets may be appropriate. See Comment 6 to 1999 § 9-401.

§ 10. Rights Between Parties Where Security Interest Is Assigned

a. *Right to Assign; Prohibition of Assignment Ineffective*

Sometimes a security interest (and the right to

payment of the debt secured by the security interest) is assigned or transferred to a third person who, as assignee, becomes the secured party.   Such an assignment is frequently contemplated in cases where a seller of goods on credit takes a purchase-money security interest and then assigns that interest to a bank or finance company.   Such a purchase-money security interest normally gives rise to *chattel paper* (conditional sales agreement) wherein the buyer gives the seller a security interest in the goods sold.   The chattel paper is then assigned by the seller to the bank or finance company.

Assignments are also often made of *accounts* or *general intangibles* which are rights to payment of money.   In short, accounts, general intangibles and chattel paper may be the subject of assignment under Article 9.   The person who is obligated on such an assigned account, chattel paper or general intangible is the *account debtor*, under the definition in 1999 § 9-102(a)(3).   Where there is a sale (including an assignment without recourse) of an account or chattel paper, the transaction is within the scope of Article 9.   1999 § 9-109(a)(3).   See Chapter 1, § 4.

The rights between the various parties, the account debtor, the assignor and the assignee, are dealt with in 1999 §§ 9-404 – 406 which cover such matters as the availability of defenses of the account debtor against the assignee, the right of the account debtor and the assignor to modify their contract and the right of the account debtor to pay the assignor. These are dealt with in subsequent discussion in this section.

Discussed elsewhere are the effects of perfection of a security interest taken by an assignor on the rights of an assignee (see Chapter 4, § 9) and the indication of an assignment on a filed financing statement or a separate statement of assignment (see Chapter 5, § 9).

It should be noted here, however, that as to agreements between an account obligor and an assignor, or in promissory notes, under 1999 § 9-406(d)(1), an attempt therein to prohibit, restrict or require the consent of the account debtor or person obligated on a promissory note to the assignment or transfer or, or the creation, attachment, perfection, or enforcement of a security interest in, is ineffective with respect to an account, chattel paper, payment intangible, or promissory note.

Former Comment 4 to 1972 § 9-318 pointed out that, in theory, such a prohibition was given effect under prior law, but that in practice most courts construed purported prohibitions of assignments in such manner as to be ineffective. See also Comment 5 to 1999 § 9-406.

b. Right of Account Debtor to Assert Defense Against Assignee

Unless an account debtor has made an enforceable agreement not to assert defenses or claims against an assignee, the account debtor may assert such defenses or claims under circumstances set forth at 1999 § 9-404. Under 1999 § 9-404(a) (1), the rights of the assignee are subject to all terms of the agreement between the account debtor and the assignor and any defense or claim in recoupment arising from the transaction that gave rise to the contract. "Recoupment" is the legal ability to subtract from any payment due the amount the person trying to collect the debt (or that person's predecessor) happens to owe the debtor. See Comment 3 to 1990 § 3-305. Under 1999 § 9-404(a) (2), the rights of an assignee also are subject to any other defenses or claims of the account debtor against the assignor which accrues before the account debtor receives a notification of the assignment authenticated by the assignor or the assignee.

Example 1. A entered into a contract with B for B to construct a building on A's land. B assigned their right to payment from A to C for a loan made by C to B. C notified A to make all payments due under the contract to C. When B failed to complete the construction, A withheld the final payment under the contract. C has no claim against A. Moreover, if A had made the final payment to C before learning that B had abandoned the job, A could recover the payment from C as having been made by mistake, where C had not changed their position after receiving payment (as by making an additional loan to B).

Example 2. On April 1, Buyer entered into a contract with Seller for delivery by Seller of a quantity of widgets on June 1. On May 1, Buyer entered into a second contract with Seller for delivery by Seller immediately of another quantity of widgets. Seller assigned the amount due under the latter contract to Bank on May 2 and delivered the widgets to Buyer that same day. Bank notified Buyer of assignment of the amount under the second contract. Seller failed to make delivery on June 1 under the first contract. Buyer asserted a setoff against the payment due Bank under the assignment of the second contract for damages arising from Seller's breach of the first contract. The setoff may not be made, since the claim accrued on June 1 after Buyer had been notified of the assignment, and arose under a contract independent of the one assigned.

The 1999 Code does provide some qualifications to the general rule discussed above that an assignee is subject to the claims and defenses of the account debtor. In general, the claim of an account debtor against an assignor may be asserted against an assignee only to reduce the amount the account debtor owes. 1999 § 9-404(b). However, a separate consumer protection law that provides otherwise will preempt. 1999 § 9-404(c). Also as to consumer account debtors, 1999 § 9-404(d) preserves the effectiveness of the notice required by the Federal Trade Commission to the effect that defenses and claims of the consumer are preserved and are assertable against an assignee, including a claim that would lead to affirmative recovery. See Comment 4 to 1999 § 9-404(d). Finally, 1999 § 9-404 does not apply to an assignment of healthcare insurance receivables. 1999 § 9-404(e).

c. Waiver of Defenses Against Assignee

The 1999 Code validates an agreement between an account debtor and an assignor not to assert against an assignee any claim or defense that the account debtor may have against the assignor if the assignee takes the assignment for value, in good faith, without notice of a claim of a property or possessory right to the property assigned, and without notice of a defense or claim in recoupment of the type that may be asserted against a person entitled to enforce a negotiable instrument under 1990 § 3-305(a). See 1999 § 9-403(b). This is an exception to the general rule set forth in 1999 § 9-404(a) that the rights of an assignee are subject to a defense or claim arising between the account debtor and the assignor. The 1999 Code also makes it clear that in any event the assignee is subject to the so-called real defenses that are assertable against a holder in due course of a negotiable instrument under 1990 § 3-305(a)(1), (b). Additionally, separate consumer protection law is given preemptive effect. See 1999 § 9-403(d), (e) and Comments 5 and 6 to 1999 § 9-403.

Example 1. Debtor purchased equipment from Seller and signed a conditional sales contract for the unpaid price. The contract did not contain a "waiver of defense" clause and was not accompanied by a negotiable note. Seller assigned the conditional sales contract to Financer. The equipment did not operate properly and was worthless to Debtor. Debtor may refuse to pay Financer the amount due under the assigned contract. On the other hand, if the assigned contract had contained a "waiver of defense" clause in favor of any assignee or had been accompanied by a negotiable promissory note or other instrument, Debtor would be barred from asserting the defense against Financer if the latter had taken for value, in good faith and without notice of a claim or defense.

Example 2. Debtor-farmer purchased a tractor from Seller and signed a conditional sales contract which contained a waiver of defense clause in favor of any assignee. The clause is effective to bar a defense asserted because the tractor is defective. The tractor is not consumer goods. This assumes that any subsequent assignee gave value for the assignment and took in good faith without notice of the defense.

Example 3. Debtor purchased consumer goods from Seller on a conditional sales contract which contained a clause stating: "Debtor agrees to settle all claims against Seller directly with Seller and will not set up any such claims against Seller as defense, counterclaim, set off, cross complaint or otherwise in any action for the purchase price or possession of the collateral brought by any assignee of this contract." Seller assigned the contract to Financer. There is consumer protection law protecting buyers of consumer goods notwithstanding use of a "waiver of defense" clause in a conditional sales agreement. Buyer may assert a defense of nondelivery of the consumer goods.

d. Right of Account Debtor and Assignor to Modify Contract

Pre-Code law was in confusion as to whether modification of an executory contract by an account debtor and an assignor without the assignee's consent was possible after notification of an assignment.

Under the 1999 Code, a modification or a substitution for an assigned contract is effective against an assignee if made in good faith. 1999 § 9-405(a). This is the case to the extent that the right to payment or a part thereof under an assigned contract has not been fully earned by performance or the right to payment or a part thereof has been fully earned by performance and the account debtor has not received notice of the assignment. 1999 § 9-405(b); see also 1999 § 9-406(a). However, the 1999 Code gives preemptive effect to consumer protection law outside the Code and also makes 1999 § 9-405 inapplicable to an assignment of a health-care-insurance receivable. 1999 § 9-405(c), (d).

Example. A has a prime contract with the government for A to manufacture gadgets. A enters into a subcontract with B for the latter to manufacture widgets, which are parts used in the manufacture of gadgets. B assigns payments due from A under the subcontract to financer C. The government subsequently exercises its right to modify the prime contract by reducing the quantity of gadgets ordered from A. A enters into a corresponding modification with B under the subcontract reducing the quantity of widgets to be delivered by B. The modification is binding on C. However, the modification only affects executory rights and cannot cut off a right of C to collect assigned amounts due from A to B for widgets already delivered by B to A. See former Comment 2 to 1972 § 9-318 for discussion of problems arising in connection with government contracts upon which this Example is based.

e. *Right of Account Debtor to Pay Assignor*

Under the 1999 Code, an account debtor on an account, chattel paper, or a payment intangible may discharge its obligation by paying the assignor until the account debtor receives an authenticated notice of the assignment. 1999 § 9-406(a). The 1999 Code specifies when the notice is effective [1999 § 9-406(b)] and that the account debtor can require proof of the assignment [1999 § 9-406(c)]. Separate consumer protection law is given preemptive effect [1999 § 9-406(h)] and § 9-406 indicates that it is inapplicable to assignment of health-care-insurance receivables [1999 § 9-406(i)].

CHAPTER 4

PERFECTION OF SECURITY INTEREST

§ 1. Perfection Generally

"[A] security interest is perfected if it has attached and all the applicable requirements for perfection ... have been satisfied." 1999 § 9-308(a).

Although *attachment* of a security interest with or without perfection is necessary to give a secured party rights in the collateral against the debtor, a secured party may maximize their rights against third persons having claims to the collateral by taking whatever action is necessary to *perfect* their interest. A secured party with an attached but unperfected security interest has but limited rights against third persons.

"A perfected security interest may still be or become subordinate to other interests.... However, in general, after perfection the secured party is protected against creditors and transferees of the debtor and, in particular, against any representative of creditors in insolvency proceedings instituted by or against the debtor." 1999 § 9-308, Comment 2.

In other words, the holder of a perfected security interest is able in most circumstances to realize on the collateral against the claim of a subsequent lien creditor or a representative of creditors such as a receiver, an assignee for the benefit of creditors, or a bankruptcy trustee. As to the rights of the secured party when the debtor is in bankruptcy, see Chapter 8. Moreover, such a perfected security interest is superior to the security interest of a third person in the same collateral which is not perfected or which is subsequently perfected, although there are certain exceptions to this rule. In addition, a perfected security interest has priority over buyers of the collateral, although some classes of buyers prevail over even a perfected security interest.

Various methods exist for the perfection of a security interest. In all cases, perfection cannot take place before the security interest has attached under 1999 § 9-308(a), and additional steps often must be taken to perfect before or after the security interest has attached. The particular method which is effective to perfect a security interest depends on the kind of personal property serving as collateral in the secured transaction, and sometimes on the nature of the transaction itself. The various methods of perfection under the 1999 version of Article 9 (discussed in detail in this chapter) are as follows:

(1) automatic perfection when the security interest attaches;

(2) temporary perfection;

(3) perfection through a pledge or the secured party taking possession of the collateral;

(4) the filing of a financing statement in one or more public filing offices (Note that this is the most common method of perfection. Filing is discussed at § 5 of this chapter and is considered in detail in Chapter 5.);

(5) filing or registration or compliance with a certificate of title requirement pursuant to federal law or a treaty;

(6) compliance with a state certificate of title law or central filing under a state statute other than the Uniform Commercial Code;

(7) taking the necessary steps to perfect with respect to investment property;

(8) perfection by "control";

(9) perfection as to agricultural liens;

(10) perfection as to "true" consignments;

(11) perfection when a sale and assignment of

payment intangibles and a sale of promissory notes occurs;

(12) perfection as to commercial tort claims;

(13) perfection as to "supporting obligations";

(14) perfection when an assignment of a "healthcare-insurance receivable occurs;

(15) perfection as to instruments.

§ 2. Perfection Upon Attachment Alone

a. *Purchase-Money Security Interest in Consumer Goods*

In certain instances, it is not necessary that any steps be taken to perfect a security interest other than attachment of that interest. In other words, with respect to certain kinds of collateral, a security interest is automatically perfected when it attaches. No action such as filing or the taking of possession of the collateral is necessary.

The most significant type of security interest which is automatically perfected upon attachment alone is a *purchase-money security interest in consumer goods* (with certain exceptions if the consumer goods are fixtures or motor vehicles). See 1999 §§ 9-310(b)(2) and 9-309(1). (Note that the definition of *purchase-money security interest* is considered in Chapter 1, § 9c(2). The definition of *consumer good*s is considered in Chapter 1, § 7a.) This follows the rule of many jurisdictions under pre-Code law which did not make security interests in consumer goods arising from conditional sales or bailment leases subject to filing requirements. See former 1972 § 9-302 Comment 4.

The policy behind this rule is that it is sometimes unwise to require filing where the benefits of public filing are outweighed by the disadvantages of filing with respect to a large number of transactions involving rather small amounts of credit and collateral of relatively low value. Filing for such transactions merely clutters the files, inconveniences those involved in the filing process and may result in expenses for filing fees disproportionate to amounts of credit given.

Although purchase-money security interests in consumer goods are perfected without filing, it should be noted that filing with respect to such collateral is permitted on an optional basis. Under 1999 § 9-320(b), unless a financing statement is filed, a third person who buys consumer goods from the consumer-debtor may take free of the security interest even though perfected, if the third person also uses the goods for consumer purposes. See

1999 § 9-320 Comment 5.

It should be kept in mind that 1999 §§ 9-309(1), 9-311(a) and (b) require filing if the consumer goods is a motor vehicle required to be registered, and a fixture filing is required for priority over conflicting interests in fixtures to the extent provided in 1999 § 9-334. In other words, if the collateral is a motor vehicle purchased for personal or family use, a security interest may be perfected only by filing or by complying with a state certificate of title law. The same may be true under 1999 § 9-311(a)(2) with respect to such consumer goods as boats, trailers or mobile homes subject to a state certificate of title law. If the consumer goods collateral is a fixture (such as a furnace affixed in a dwelling house), a security interest may be perfected by attachment but fixture filing is necessary in order to obtain priority over certain real estate interests.

Example 1. Buyer purchases a combination stereo-television set from Seller on installment credit for personal, family or household purposes. The purchase is made under a written security agreement. The set is delivered to Buyer's home. Upon delivery, the security interest attaches and is perfected upon attachment. If Seller assigns the security interest to Financer, the security interest continues perfected. See 1999 §§ 9-310(b)(2), 9-

309(1), and 9-310(c).

Example 2. Under the facts of Example 1, Seller sells the set for cash, but Buyer borrows from Financer and uses the money to pay Seller. The security interest is perfected in favor of Financer upon attachment, since Financer has a purchase-money security interest. See 1999 §§ 9-103, 9-310(b)(2), 9-309(1).

Example 3. Buyer purchases an automobile from Dealer on installment credit for personal, family or household purposes. The purchase is made under a written security agreement. The car is delivered to Buyer. Upon delivery, the security interest attaches but is not perfected unless a financing statement is filed or there is compliance with an applicable state certificate-of-title law. See 1999 §§ 9-309(1), 9-311(b)(2).

Example 4. Buyer purchases a furnace from Seller on installment credit for personal, family or household purposes. The purchase is made under a written security agreement. The furnace is installed as a fixture in Buyer's home. Under 1999 § 9-309(1), the security interest is perfected upon attachment, but a fixture filing is necessary for priority over certain real estate interests under 1999 § 9-334.

b. Isolated Assignments of Accounts

1999 §§ 9-309(2) and 9-310(b)(2) provide that filing is not necessary to perfect a security interest in an assignment of accounts which does not alone or in conjunction with other assignments to the same assignee transfer a significant part of the outstanding accounts of the assignor.

The effect of 1999 § 9-309(2) is to permit perfection upon attachment alone with respect to isolated assignments of accounts. This rule is justified on the ground that casual or isolated assignments which no one would think of filing should not be subject to invalidation by reason of failure to file. On the other hand, any person who regularly takes assignments of a particular debtor's accounts should file. See Comment 4 to 1999 § 9-309.

Example. Assignor assigned accounts totaling $6,000 to Assignee for a cash consideration of $4,000. At that time, Assignor was doing about $10,000 worth of business every month. The assignment gave Assignee a perfected security interest in the accounts without the necessity of filing.

It should also be noted that 1999 §§ 9-109(d)(4)-(7) completely exclude certain transfers of accounts from Article 9. See discussion of exclusions in

Chapter 1, § 5.

c. Other Instances

In certain other instances, a security interest may be perfected without filing. Such perfection takes place with respect to the following kinds of collateral:

(1) Temporary perfection as to instruments, certificated securities, negotiable documents, or goods in possession of a bailee other than one who has issued a negotiable document of title, for not over 20 days or in proceeds for not over 20 days. See 1999 §§ 9-312(e)-(h) and 9-315(d). See discussion of temporary perfection in the next section of this chapter.

(2) A security interest created by an assignment of a beneficial interest in a decedent's estate. 1999 § 9-309(13).

(3) A security interest of a collecting bank in an item taken for collection (such as a check taken on deposit when the bank permits the depositor to withdraw the proceeds before the check is collected). 1999 § 9-309(7).

(4) A security interest arising under Article 2 of the Code on Sales or Article 2A of the Code on

Leases where the debtor-buyer/lessee does not have possession of the goods. 1999 § 9-309(6).

(5) A security interest in investment property created by a broker or a securities intermediary or in a commodity contract or a commodity account created by a commodity intermediary. 1999 § 9-309(10), (11).

(6) An assignment for the benefit of all the creditors of the transferor, and subsequent transfers by the assignee thereunder. 1999 § 9-309(12).

§ 3. Temporary Perfection in Certain Collateral

The 1999 Code indicates that a security interest in certificated securities, negotiable documents, or instruments is perfected without filing or the taking of possession for a period of 20 days from the time it attaches.   However, the temporary perfection applies only to the extent the security interest arises for new value given under an authenticated security agreement. 1999 § 9-312(e).

The 1999 Code also provides for temporary perfection in goods or documents made available to the debtor under some circumstances. 1999 §9-312(f).   Specifically, the provision applies to a perfected security interest in a negotiable document or goods in possession of a bailee, other than one who has issued a negotiable document for the goods. The security interest remains perfected for 20 days without filing if the secured party makes available to the debtor the goods or documents representing the goods for either of two purposes. One purpose is to facilitate the sale or exchange of the goods or documents. The second purpose is to facilitate loading, unloading, storing, shipping, trans-shipping, manufacturing, processing or otherwise dealing with them in a manner preliminary to their sale or exchange. Similarly, a perfected security interest in a certificated security or instrument remains perfected for 20 days without filing if the secured party delivers the certificate or instrument to the debtor for the purpose of ultimate sale or exchange or presentment, collection, enforcement, renewal, or registration of transfer. 1999 § 9-312(g).

Finally, after the 20-day periods described above expire, the secured party must take steps to otherwise perfect the security interest to maintain perfection 1999 § 9-312(h).

§ 4. Perfection by Pledge or Possessory Security Interest

a. Generally

The kinds of personal property which may be the subject of a pledge or possessory security interest are listed in Chapter 1, § 9a. Such items include goods and collateral represented by a writing that may transfer a claim through delivery or through delivery plus indorsement. A writing capable of transferring the claim may be an instrument, a document or chattel paper. On the other hand, purely intangible collateral such as accounts and chattel paper cannot be pledged. Perfection as to such collateral is only by filing, although in certain instances there may be automatic perfection as to isolated accounts or perfection as proceeds. See 1999 §§ 9-309(2) and 9-315(a), (c)-(e). Note that investment property, including a certificated security, is not included within the definition of "instrument." As to security interests in investment property, see § 4b of this chapter and Chapter 1, § 9a(3).

With respect to collateral that may be pledged, a security interest is perfected without filing if the collateral is in the possession of the secured party. See 1999 §§ 9-310(b)(6) and 9-313. For discussion of perfection of security interests in instruments under the 1999 Code, see § 12h of this chapter. In addition, under the 1999 Code, a security interest in money may be perfected only by possession except where the money is proceeds. See 1999 § 9-312(b)(3).

The common law rules on the degree and extent of possession which are necessary to perfect a pledge interest are not relaxed by any provision of Article 9. See Comment 3 to 1999 § 9-205. Possession may be by the secured party or by an agent on their behalf, but it is clear that *the debtor or a person controlled by them cannot qualify as such an agent for the secured party.* See Comment 3 to 1999 § 9-313 and also 1999 § 9-205(b).

b. Investment Property

The 1972 version of Article 9 was significantly amended regarding security interests in investment securities and the like in 1994. These amendments changed the method by which secured transactions in such collateral are structured.

The 1999 version of Article 9 follows the 1994 amendments to the 1972 version of Article 9 and, thus, does not substantially change how a secured transaction should be structured under the 1994 amendments to obtain perfection of a security interest in investment property. The 1994 amendments, which involved changes both to Article 8 and to the 1972 Article 9, dealt not only with stocks and bonds represented by physical pieces of paper, known as *certificated securities* [see § 8-102(a)(4)], but also with similar rights against an issuing corporation that are evidenced by a registration in a computer at the corporation, known as *uncertificated securities* [see § 8-102(a)(18)]. The amendments also recognized the current method of holding securities in an account with a stockbroker in which the stockholder's ownership is reflected merely by a bookkeeping entry in the stockbroker's records, known as a *securities entitlement* [see § 8-102(a)(17)]. The 1994 amendments to Article 9 combined these methods of owning securities with similar ownership rights in commodity contracts and accounts. The 1994 Code referred to all such property as *investment property.* See § 9-115 (1972 version as amended in 1994). The 1999 Article 9 continues use of the same term. See § 9-102(a)(49).

There are essentially two methods of structuring a secured transaction in investment property. One method does not involve taking possession or control of the investment property by the secured party; rather the secured party, after attaching the security interest, will file a financing statement. See 1999 § 9-312(a). Under the second method, the secured party takes "control" of the investment property. See 1999 § 9-314(a). There are different ways to take control of the investment property. For example, a secured party has control over a certificated security by taking possession of it, along with any necessary indorsements. See §§ 8-106(a), (b) and 8-301(a). As to uncertificated securities, the secured party takes control by being registered as the owner of the stock in the records of the issuing corporation or takes other steps to make certain that it can reach the rights of the debtor in the event it needs to enforce the security interest. The other steps include, for example, having a stockbrokerage account of the debtor changed such that the secured party is the owner or entering an agreement with the stockbroker and the debtor whereby they agree to honor the order of the secured party regarding disposition of the investment property should the debtor default. See §§ 8-106(c) and (d). To insure priority of investment property generally as against other claimants, it is best to acquire control of the investment property as opposed to filing a financing statement. The Code gives to a controlling secured party priority over another secured party who has only filed a financing statement. See 1999 § 9-328.

c. Where Collateral Is Held by Bailee

If collateral is held by a third person as bailee, the secured party is deemed to have possession under some circumstances, and is thereby perfected. See 1999 § 9-313(c). Under the 1999 Code, with respect to collateral other than certificated securities and goods covered by a document of title, the secured party takes possession only when the third-person bailee has authenticated a record that acknowledges it holds the collateral for the secured party's benefit. See 1999 § 9-313(c) and Comment 4.

It should also be noted that during the period that goods are in the possession of the issuer of a negotiable document [such as a warehouseman who has issued a negotiable warehouse receipt or a carrier that has issued a negotiable bill of lading], a security interest in the goods is perfected by perfecting a security interest in the document. See 1999 § 9-312(c). This provision takes the position that so long as a negotiable document covering goods is outstanding, title to the goods is locked up in the document and the proper way of dealing with the goods is through the document. Moreover, a security interest taken on the goods themselves while a negotiable document is outstanding is subordinate to a security interest taken in the document.

A debtor may pledge a negotiable document to a secured party and thus give the latter a perfected security interest in the goods, as well as in the document. See 1999 § 9-312(c).

Similarly, the Code provides that a secured party may perfect a security interest in investment property, i.e. stocks, by the giving of notice (through an agreement) to a third person (such as a bank, broker, or other person) who is in possession or control of the stock and is in an analogous position to that of a bailee. Generally, as to security interests in investment property, see § 4b of this chapter and Chapter 1, § 9a(3).

§ 5. Perfection by Filing

Generally, perfection as to most kinds of collateral is accomplished by filing a financing statement in a public office. See 1999 § 9-310(a) which states that a financing statement must be filed to perfect all security interests, with certain exceptions discussed in the preceding sections of this chapter. As to the details of filing, including where to file and what to file, see Chapter 5.

In many instances, a security interest may be perfected either by filing or by possession. This applies to goods, chattel paper or negotiable documents. See 1999 §§ 9-310(b)(6) and 9-313. Under the 1999 Code, filing is effective to perfect a security interest even in instruments, but the creditor must take possession of money to perfect a security interest therein. See 1999 §§ 9-312(a) and 9-312(b)(3). Conversely, filing is the only general means of perfecting a security interest in accounts and general intangibles, although there are exceptions as to isolated accounts under 1999 § 9-309(2), as to assignment of an interest in an estate under 1999 § 9-309(13) (estates only), and as to an assignment for the benefit of creditors under 1999 § 9-309(12).

As indicated above, as to investment property, i.e. stocks, filing is a permissible means of perfection, although taking "control" of the investment property is a better method of perfection because it gives the secured party a better priority position in the collateral. See 1999 § 9-328(1). For discussion of perfection of security interests in investment property, see § 4b of this chapter and Chapter 1, § 9a(3).

In certain instances, the filing requirements may be complied with by registration or filing pursuant to a statute or treaty of the United States, by central filing under a state statute or by compliance with an applicable certificate of title law. See 1999 § 9-311.

See also discussion in the next two sections of this chapter.

§ 6. Perfection Where Filing is Required Under Federal Law

The filing provisions of Article 9 do not apply where the collateral is subject to a requirement of federal law under which there is a national registration or filing or a national certificate of title. Compliance with such federal requirement is equivalent to filing under Article 9. See 1999 § 9-311(a)(1), (b). The 1999 Code makes it clear that compliance with a treaty providing for international registration or an international certificate of title has the effect of filing under Article 9.

Filing or registration under a federal statute may be made with respect to such property as copyrights, trademarks, patents, aircraft, and rolling stock of a railroad. Where such filing requirements exist, they must be complied with for perfection, and filing under Article 9 is ineffective. On the other hand, where the security interest consists of the assignment of a claim against the United States, it is necessary both to file under Article 9 and to comply with the federal Assignment of Claims Act, which requires the giving of notice to contracting and disbursing officers and to sureties on bonds, but does not establish a national filing system. See Comment 2 to 1999 § 9-311.

§ 7. Compliance With State Certificate-of-Title Law or Other Filing Requirement

The filing provisions of Article 9 do not apply where the collateral is subject to a state certificate-of-title law under which it is required that a security interest be indicated on a certificate of title or under which central filing is required under a state statute other than the Uniform Commercial Code. Compliance with such a certificate-of-title law or other state statute is equivalent to filing under Article 9. See 1999 §§ 9-310(b)(3), 9-311(a)(2), (3). Filing is not required to perfect a security interest in property subject to enumerated certificate-of-title statutes, except during the time when the goods are inventory held by a dealer for sale. 1999 § 9-311(d).

The major items of collateral subject to certificate- of-title laws which provide for indication of a security interest are motor vehicles, in probably the majority of states. However, filing is necessary with respect to motor vehicles in "nontitle" states (or states which do not have certificate-of-title laws providing for indication of a security interest on such a certificate as the means of perfecting a security interest). The certificate-of-title laws do not apply where motor vehicles are inventory held by a dealer for sale.

In some states, other items of collateral are also subject to certificate-of-title laws, such as boats.

Under 1999 § 9-311(a)(3), filing is not necessary where there is compliance with a certificate-of-title law of another state under the law of which indication of a security interest on the certificate is required as a condition of perfection.

The Code provides in 1999 § 9-311(a)(2), (b) that filing under the Code is not necessary where the property is subject to a statute (separate from the UCC) of the state which provides for central filing. This has the effect of permitting filing where the debtor is a transmitting utility under a central filing statute, and such is clear under the Code which has provisions for central filing where the debtor is a transmitting utility.

§ 8.   Perfection as to Proceeds

"Proceeds" includes whatever is received upon the sale, exchange, collection or other disposition of collateral or proceeds.   1999 § 9-102(a)(64).   See discussion of proceeds as collateral in Chapter 1, § 7d. Under 1999 § 9-315(a)(2), a security interest in collateral which is sold, exchanged or otherwise disposed of attaches to any identifiable proceeds.

The perfection of security interests in proceeds under the 1999 Code is dealt with in 1999 § 9-315. Under the 1999 Code, it is not necessary to specifically file as to proceeds or make a specific reference to proceeds in a financing statement. In most instances, a filing as to collateral automatically covers proceeds and no action is necessary to perfect as to proceeds. See 1999 § 9-315(c), which provides that a security interest in proceeds is a perfected security interest if the security interest in the original collateral was perfected. The 1999 Code does provide that a perfected security interest in proceeds becomes unperfected on the 21st day after the security interest attaches to the proceeds unless one of three conditions are satisfied. See 1999 § 9-315(d).

First, under the 1999 Code the security interest in proceeds continues to be perfected beyond 20 days of attachment if a filed financing statement covers the original collateral, the proceeds are collateral in which a security interest may be perfected by filing in the office(s) in which the financing statement has been filed, and the proceeds are not acquired with cash proceeds. 1999 § 9-315(d)(1).

Second, under the 1999 Code the security interest in proceeds continues to be perfected beyond 20 days of attachment if the proceeds are identifiable cash proceeds. 1999 § 9-315(d)(2).

Finally, under the 1999 Code the security interest in proceeds continues to be perfected beyond 20 days of attachment if the security interest in the proceeds is perfected other than under 1999 § 9-315(c) when the security interest attaches to the proceeds or within 20 days thereafter. 1999 § 9-315(d)(3). This provision requires the secured party to take action in order to perfect the security interest when such perfection does not occur because the security interest in the original collateral was not perfected.

§ 9. Perfection When Security Interest is Assigned.

If a secured party assigns a perfected security interest, no filing is required in order to continue the perfected status of the security interest against creditors of and transferees from the original debtor. 1999 § 9-310(c).

Example. Buyer buys goods from Seller who retains a security interest in them which they perfect (as by filing or even without filing if it is a purchase-money security interest in consumer goods). Seller assigns the perfected security interest to X. The security interest, in X's hands and without further steps on their part, continues perfected against *Buyer's* transferees and creditors. If, however, the assignment from Seller to X was itself intended for security (or was a sale of accounts or chattel paper), X must take whatever steps may be required in order to be protected against *Seller's* creditors. See Comment 4 to 1999 § 9-310.

Although a secured transaction perfected against the original debtor by filing need not be further filed by an assignee of the security interest, it should be noted that 1999 § 9-514 provides for the disclosing of an assignment in a financing statement and also provide for the filing of a separate written statement of assignment. Such filings as to an assignment are generally permitted on an optional basis, but are necessary when a continuation statement, statement of release, or termination statement is presented for filing signed by one other than the secured party of record. For discussion of filing when there is an assignment, see Chapter 5, § 9.

§ 10. Time of Perfection

When perfection occurs by possession, the 1999 Code provides that "[i]f perfection of a security interest depends upon possession of the collateral by the secured party, perfection occurs no earlier than the time the secured party takes possession and continues only while the secured party retains possession." 1999 § 9-313(d). See also 1999 § 9-313(e) as to certificated securities in registered form.

In other instances, under the 1999 Code the time of perfection is determined by the time the security interest attaches and when all of the applicable steps required for perfection have been taken. See 1999 § 9-308(a). Thus, where a security interest has attached and perfection is by filing, the time of perfection is generally the time of filing. In this connection, the 1999 Code indicates that communication of a record to a filing office and tender of the filing fee or acceptance of the record by the filing office constitutes filing. 1999 § 9-516(a).

If the steps necessary to perfection are taken before the security interest attaches, the security interest is perfected at the time when it attaches. 1999 § 9-308(a).

Example. Secured party files a financing statement before giving value, before a written security agreement is executed or before the debtor has rights in the collateral. The security interest is perfected automatically if and when it attaches. See Comment 2 to 1999 § 9-308.

§ 11. Continuity of Perfection

The Code takes the position that perfection is continuous where it occurs through different methods and where there is no intervening period when the perfection is lost. In other words, if a security interest is originally perfected in any way permitted under Article 9 and is subsequently perfected in some other way under Article 9, without an intermediate period when it was unperfected, the security interest is deemed to be perfected continuously. See 1999 § 9-308(c).

Example 1. Debtor gives possession of certain goods to Creditor in pledge (such as in a field warehousing transaction) to secure a loan. Later, Creditor files a financing statement and then relinquishes possession of the goods to Debtor. Creditor's security interest was perfected first by possession and then by filing without an intermediate period when it was unperfected. Creditor's security interest was continuously perfected from the time possession was originally taken.

Example 2. Bank which has issued a letter of credit honors drafts drawn under the credit and receives possession of a negotiable bill of lading covering the goods shipped. Under 1999 §§ 9-312(f) and 9-313, Bank has a perfected security interest in the document and the goods. Bank releases the bill of lading to Debtor for the purpose of the latter procuring the goods from the carrier and selling them. Under 1999 § 9-312(f), Bank continues to have a perfected security interest in the document or goods for 20 days. Bank files before the expiration of the 20-day period. Its security interest continues perfected for as long as the filing is good. When the goods are sold by Debtor, Bank continues to have a security interest in the proceeds of the sale to the extent stated in 1999 § 9-315.

§ 12. Additional Methods of Perfection Provided for in the 1999 Code

The 1999 Code added some perfection methods not found in the 1972 Code. Some of the added "methods" actually relate to additional forms of collateral that fall within the 1999 Code's scope of application that were not included in the 1972 Code. These methods of perfecting a security interest are discussed below.

a. Perfection by "Control."

The 1999 Code created a perfection method based upon the secured party acquiring control of the collateral. The control perfection method applies to collateral that is a deposit account [1999 § 9-102(a)(29)], letter-of-credit right [1999 § 9-102(a)(51)], electronic chattel paper [1999 § 9-102(a)(31)] or investment property [1999 § 9-102(a)(49)]. Specifically, the 1999 Code provides that a security interest in such collateral may be perfected by control of the collateral. 1999 § 9-314(a).

Control of deposit accounts is acquired if the secured party is the bank with which the deposit is maintained or if the debtor, secured party and bank have agreed in an authenticated record that the bank will comply with the secured party's instructions regarding disposition of the account funds, or if the secured party becomes the account holder, that is, the secured party becomes the bank's customer with respect to the account. 1999 § 9-104. Control of electronic chattel paper is acquired essentially by the secured party being identified as the assignee of the chattel paper on the record of the secured party. 1999 § 9-105. As to a letter-of-credit right, the 1999 Code indicates that the secured party has control essentially if the issuer has consented to an assignment of the letter-of-credit proceeds. 1999 § 9-107;

see also UCC § 5-114(c). The 1999 Code emphasizes that a security interest perfected by control in these collateral types remains perfected only while the secured party retains control. 1999 § 9-314(a) and (b).

Obtaining control of investment property is treated somewhat differently. For discussion of perfection of security interests in investment property, see § 4b of this chapter and Chapter 1, § 9a(3).

b. Agricultural Liens

The 1999 Article 9 included agricultural liens within its scope of coverage. See 1999 § 9-109(a)(2). "Agricultural lien" is defined in the Code at 1999 § 9-102(a)(5). Essentially, an agricultural lien is an interest other than a security interest in farm products created by statute for one who sells goods or services in the ordinary course of business to a farmer or rents real property to a farmer who uses it in connection with a farming operation. The interest, of course, secures payment of debts the farmer-debtor incurs for the purchase of the goods or services and lease of the real property. To be an "agricultural lien" the 1999 Code also provides that the effectiveness of the lien must not depend on the person's possession of the personal property. Agricultural liens are statutory liens that are drawn in the 1999 Code for perfection and priority purposes. As to perfection of an agricultural lien, the lienor must file a financing statement. 1999 §§ 9-310(a), 9-308(b).

c. *"True" Consignments*

A significant change regarding consignment transactions was made under the 1999 version of Article 9. The 1999 Article flatly states that the Article applies to consignments. See 1999 § 9-109(a)(4). The 1999 Article § 9-102(a)(20) defines "consignment" as a transaction, regardless of its form, in which a person delivers goods to a merchant for the purpose of sale. The merchant must deal in goods of this kind under a name other than the name of the person making delivery and must not be an auctioneer and the merchant must not generally be known by its creditors to be substantially engaged in selling goods of others. See 1999 § 9-102(a)(20)(A). The aggregate value of the goods must be $1,000 or more at the time of delivery. See 1999 § 9-102(a)(20)(B). The goods must not be consumer goods immediately before delivery [1999 § 9-102(a)(20)(C)] and the transaction must not create a security interest that secures an obligation [1999 § 9-

102(a)(20))(D)].

The gist of the 1999 changes is that some "true" consignments (as described above) that are bailments of goods for the purpose of sale by the bailee, are within the scope of UCC Article 9. In most consignment transactions, the consignor should file a financing statement in order to protect its interest against creditors of the consignee. See 1999 §§ 9-310(a), 9-102(a)(20), 9-109(a)(4).

d. Sales and Assignments of Payment Intangibles and Sales of Promissory Notes.

The 1999 Code also created a new classification of collateral termed "payment intangibles." The 1999 Code defines a payment intangible as meaning a "general intangible" under which the account debtor's principal obligation is a monetary obligation. 1999 § 9-102(a)(61). The term "promissory note" also is defined by the 1999 Code which gives it its ordinary meaning. 1999 § 102 (a)(65). As to perfection of security interests in such collateral, the 1999 Code flatly provides that the security interest is automatically perfected when a security interest attaches and the collateral is sold. 1999 § 9-309(3), (4). See also Comment 4, 1999 § 9-309. As to payment intangibles, the 1999 Code also provides that an assignment of a payment intangible which does not by itself or in conjunction with other assignments to the same assignee transfer a significant part of the assignor's payment intangibles is automatically perfected when the security interest attaches. 1999 § 9-309(2). The upshot of all this is that a buyer of payment intangibles or promissory notes, and an assignee of payment intangibles that are not a significant part of the assignor's payment intangibles need not file a financing statement.

e. Commercial Tort Claims

The 1999 Code narrowed the 1972 Code's exclusion from Article 9 of transfers of interests in tort claims. 1972 § 9-104(k). The 1999 Code creates a new category of collateral termed "commercial tort claims," thus including such claims within its scope. A commercial tort claim is a claim that arises out of the debtor's business or profession. It does not include claims for personal injury or death of an individual. See 1999 § 9-102(a)(13). A secured party must file a financing statement to perfect its security interest in such a claim. 1999 § 9-310(a).

f. Supporting Obligations

The 1999 Code added a new form of collateral termed a "supporting obligation." A "supporting obligation" is defined at 1999 § 9-102(a)(77) to mean a letter-of-credit right or other secondary obligation such as a guaranty that supports payment or performance under an account [1999 § 9-102(a)(2)], chattel paper [1999 § 9-102(a)(11)], document [1999 § 9-102(a)(30)], general intangible [1999 § 9-102(a)(42)], instrument [1999 § 9-102(a)(47)], or investment property [1999 § 9-102(a)(49)]. A security interest in a support*ed* obligation automatically attaches to the support*ing* obligation; likewise, perfection of a security interest in the support*ed* obligation also perfects the security interest in the support*ing* obligation. 1999 §§ 9-203 (f), 9-308(d). Thus, if a secured party has a perfected security interest in a promissory note which is a type of instrument and that note is supported by a stand-by letter of credit, the secured party automatically has a perfected security interest in the letter-of-credit rights.

g. Assignment of Healthcare-Insurance Receivables

The 1999 Code created a new classification of Article 9 collateral termed "healthcare-insurance receivables." This type of collateral consists of interest in or claims under a policy of insurance which is a right to payment of a monetary obligation for healthcare goods or services. 1999 § 9-102(a) (46). The 1999 Code provides for automatic perfection of a security interest created by the assignment of the healthcare-insurance receivable to the provider of the healthcare goods or services. 1999 § 9-309(5).

h. Instruments

An "instrument" is a negotiable promissory note, draft, check or the like. 1999 § 9-102(a)(47). Traditionally, perfection of a security interest in an instrument has occurred only by the secured party taking possession of the instrument. 1972 § 9-304(1). The 1999 Code also permits perfection of a security interest in an instrument to occur by filing a financing statement. 1999 § 9-312(a). This marks a significant change in traditional practices which permit perfection of interests in an instrument only by taking possession of the instrument.

CHAPTER 5

PERFECTION OF SECURITY
INTEREST BY FILING

§ 1.   "Notice Filing"

The most common method of perfecting a security interest is by filing a financing statement in a public office. For a general discussion of perfection of a security interest by filing with respect to various kinds of collateral, see Chapter 4, § 5.

Article 9 adopts the system of "notice filing" which proved successful under the Uniform Trust Receipts Act. The basic system is explained in Comment 2 to 1999 § 9-502 as follows:

> "What is required to be filed is not, as under pre-UCC chattel mortgage and conditional sales acts, the security agreement itself, but only a simple record providing a limited amount of information (financing statement). The financing statement may be filed before the security interest attaches or thereafter....

> The notice itself indicates merely that a person may have a security interest in the collateral

indicated. Further inquiry from the parties concerned will be necessary to disclose the complete state of affairs. Section 9-210 provides a statutory procedure under which the secured party, at the debtor's request, may be required to make disclosure. However, in many cases, information may be forthcoming without the need to resort to the formalities of that section.

Notice filing has proved to be of great use in financing transactions involving inventory, accounts, and chattel paper, because it obviates the necessity of refiling on each of a series of transactions in a continuing arrangement under which the collateral changes from day to day. However, even in the case of filings that do not necessarily involve a series of transactions (e.g., a loan secured by a single item of equipment), a financing statement is effective to encompass transactions under a security agreement not in existence and not contemplated at the time the notice was filed, if the indication of collateral in the financing statement is sufficient to cover the collateral concerned. Similarly, a financing statement is effective to cover after-acquired property of the type indicated and to perfect with respect to future advances under security agreements, regardless of whether after-acquired property or future advances are mentioned in the financing statement and even if not in the contemplation of the parties at the time the financing statement was authorized to be filed."

§ 2.   Where to File

The 1999 Code provides only one approach as to the place of filing of financing statements.   The approach requires most filings to occur at a central location except for real-estate-related collateral where local filing will still occur.   Comment 2 to 1999 § 9-501 explains the reasoning that led to this change from the 1972 Code:

"Former Article 9 afforded each State three alternative approaches, depending on the extent to which the State desires central filing (usually with the Secretary of State), local filing (usually with a county office), or both. ... Local filing increases the net costs of secured transactions ... by increasing uncertainty and the number of required filings.   Any benefit that local filing may have had in the 1950's is now insubstantial. Accordingly, this Article dictates central filing for most situations, while retaining local filing for real-estate-related collateral and special filing provisions for transmitting utilities."

The 1999 Code indicates that the office in which

to file a financing statement to perfect a security interest or an agricultural lien is the office designated for filing or recording a mortgage on related real property if the collateral is as-extracted collateral [i.e., oil, gas and minerals, see 1999 § 9-102(a)(6)] or timber to be cut or the financing statement is filed as a fixture filing and the collateral is goods that are or are to become fixtures. 1999 § 9-501(a)(1). In all other cases, filing occurs in a central location as designated by each State. 1999 § 9-501 (a)(2). As to debtors that are transmitting utilities [see § 9-102(a)(80) for the definition of "transmitting utility"], filing will also occur at a designated central location, even if the collateral is fixtures. 1999 § 9-501(b). Apparently because most filings will occur centrally, the 1999 Code has no equivalent to 1972 § 9-401(2) which provides that filing in the wrong location under some circumstances will not be fatal to the effectiveness of the filing.

§ 3.   What to File: Financing Statement

The 1999 Code provisions set forth the requisite form of that which is filed, i.e., the financing statement. The following discussion will describe the form requirements.

a. Summary of 1999 Code Formal Requirements

The basic requirements of a financing statement under the 1999 Code are set forth in 1999 § 9-502(a) and (b).

The 1999 Code authorizes electronic filings; that is, the financing statement may be but need not be in tangible form. Under the 1999 Code, a "financing statement" means a record or records composed of an initial financing statement and a filed record relating to the initial financing statement. 1999 § 9-102(a)(39). A "record" means information that is inscribed as a tangible medium or which is stored in an electronic or other medium and is retrievable in perceivable form. 1999 § 9-102(a)(69).

The content requirements of financing statements are discussed in the lettered subsections which follow but are summarized here:

(1) The financing statement must provide the name of the debtor.

(2) The financing statement must provide the name of the secured party or a representative of the secured party.

(3) The financing statement must indicate the collateral covered by the financing statement.

(4) When the financing statement covers fixtures

or certain other collateral related to real estate, a description of land is necessary.

(5) The address of the parties and an indication of whether the debtor is an individual or an organization must also be included (note that the addresses and an indication of the individual/organizational status of the debtor are required by the 1999 Code but are not necessary for an initial financing statement to be legally sufficient to perfect a security interest.)

While a copy of the security agreement may be filed as a financing statement if it meets the above requirements, the normal practice is to file a simple form containing only the required information. Such a simple form is set forth in 1999 § 9-521.

The 1999 Code provides that a financing statement substantially satisfying the content requirements, summarized above, is effective even if it has minor errors or omissions, unless the errors or omissions make the financing statement seriously misleading. 1999 § 9-506(a).

Example. First Bank makes a loan to David Davis. At Bank's insistence, David Davis grants First Bank a security interest in his equipment. First Bank files a financing statement, proper in all respects except that it indicates that the name of the debtor is Douglas Davis. The error may be seriously misleading, and if it is, the filing is ineffective.

b. *Absence of Signature Requirement*

The 1999 Code does not require the debtor's signature on an initial financing statement. The purpose of eliminating the signature requirement is to accommodate electronic filings. See Comment 3 to 1999 § 9-502. The debtor authorizes filing of an initial financing statement, or an amendment that adds collateral described in the initial financing statement or a new debtor to the initial financing statement, by authenticating the security agreement. 1999 § 9-509 (a), (b). An amendment that adds collateral not covered in the security agreement or adds a new debtor must be authorized in an authenticated record. 1999 § 9-509(a).

Prior versions of Article 9 required a signature of the debtor on the financing statement. Eliminating the debtor signature requirement raised a concern that unauthorized filings might occur. That concern is addressed by the 1999 Code. Any person who files an unauthorized initial financing statement or amendment can be held liable for damages and a statutory penalty of $500. 1999 § 9-625(b), (e)(3). A filing is declared effective only to the extent it is debtor authorized. 1999 § 9-510(a). Finally, a person may file in the filing office a correction statement with respect to a record indexed there under the person's name if the person believes the record is inaccurate or was wrongfully filed. 1999 § 9-518(a). A part of the correction statement must explain the basis of the filing party's belief that the record should be corrected. 1999 § 9-518(b). This, for example, permits a purported debtor to put on public record their belief that a filed financing statement is "bogus" and should be ignored. See Comment 2 to 1999 § 9-518. On the other hand, the filing of a correction statement alone does not affect the validity of the filing it seeks to correct; the filer of the correction statement must use other legal means to affect the filing they seek to correct. See 1999 § 9-518(c) and Comment 3 to 1999 § 9-518.

Example. Carla Cook has been a long-time friend of Dale Decker. Unfortunately, the two have had a significant disagreement. To spite Decker, Cook filed a bogus financing statement indicating that Decker is the debtor. When Decker applied for a loan with Finance Company, the latter discovered the bogus filing after a routine search of the UCC filings. When Decker demanded that Cook file a termination statement, Cook refused. Decker may now file a correction statement under 1999 UCC § 9-518. However, the correction statement alone does not affect the validity of Cook's filing. Decker must use other legal means ultimately to clear up the problem. See Comment 3 to 1999 § 9-518.

c. *Naming the Parties; Effect of Name Changes and Sale of Collateral*

The 1999 Code requires that the financing statement include the name of the debtor and the name of the secured party or a representative of the secured party. 1999 § 9-502(a)(1), (2). The 1999 Code also requires a financing statement to indicate whether the debtor is an individual or an organization; failure to do so is reason for the filing officer to reject the filing, but if the filing occurs, the absence of this information does not render the financing statement legally insufficient to perfect the security interest. 1999 §§ 9-502(a), 9-516(b)(5). Because financing statements are indexed according to the debtor's name, the requirement of inclusion of the debtor's name on a financing statement is central to the notice-based filing system.

The 1999 Code indicates that if the debtor is an organization organized under state or federal law that requires maintenance of a public record indicating the organization's existence, i.e., a corporation, the financing statement must reflect the name shown on those records. 1999 §§ 9-503(a)(1), 9-102 (a)(70). There are also rules that specifically deal with naming debtors who are decedent's estates and trusts. See 1999 § 9-503(a)(2), (3).

As to all other debtors who have a name, the financing statement must provide the individual or organizational name of the debtor. 1999 §§ 9-503(a)(4)(A); 1-201(28); revised 1-201(b)(25), (27). If the debtor does not have a name, the financing statement needs to provide the names of partners, members, associates or others who comprise the debtor. 1999 § 9-503(a)(4)(B).

Under the 1999 Code, a financing statement that includes only a trade name inadequately names the debtor. 1999 § 9-503(c). On the other hand, a financing statement remains valid if it omits a trade name or the names of partners, members, or associates if the debtor has its own name. 1999 § 9-503(b). A financing statement also is effective even if it does not mention the representative capacity of the secured party or the representative of the secured party. 1999 § 9-503(d).

A financing statement that fails sufficiently to provide the name of the debtor in accordance with 1999 § 9-503(a) is deemed seriously misleading. 1999 § 9-506(b). However, if a search of the filing record under the debtor's correct name would disclose a financing statement that fails sufficiently to provide the name of the debtor in accordance with 1999 § 9-503(a), the name provided does not make the financing statement seriously misleading. 1999 § 9-506(c).

With regard to instances in which the debtor's name changes after the filing of an initial financing statement under the 1999 Code, the initial filing continues to perfect with respect to the original collateral and collateral acquired by the debtor within four months after the name change. If the name change is seriously misleading, an amendment must be filed within four months after the change to perfect the security interest in any collateral acquired beyond four months of the name change. 1999 § 9-507(c)(2).

Example. Denise Day borrowed money from Second State Bank. The loan was for Day's business. Day granted Second State Bank a security interest in all inventory, presently held and after acquired. The bank filed the financing statement. Denise subsequently married Ken Knight and changed her name to Denise Knight. Second State Bank will lose perfection of its security interest in inventory acquired by Denise beyond four months after her name change unless the bank files an amendment reflecting the change of name to Knight.

1999 § 9-507(c)(2).

The 1999 Code also deals with the effect of a sale of the collateral by the debtor. A filed financing statement remains effective with respect to collateral transferred by the debtor even if the secured party knows of or consents to the transfer. 1999 § 9-507(a). The transferee is bound by the terms of the existing security agreement if the transferee is a "new debtor." 1999 § 9-203(d). Whether one is a "new debtor" depends on the law of contracts and business organizations outside UCC Article 9. 1999 § 9-102(a)(56), (60). If the difference in names between the original and the new debtor is such that the original financing statement is now seriously misleading, the filing is effective as to the collateral transferred and any new collateral acquired during the four months after the new debtor becomes bound. 1999 § 9-508(a), (b)(1), (c). The secured party is unperfected as to new collateral acquired after the expiration of the four-month grace period unless it files an initial financing statement in the name of the new debtor. 1999 § 9-508(b)(2).

d. Addresses of Parties

Under the 1999 Code, the addresses of both the secured party and the debtor are required. However, the addresses are not necessary for an initial financing statement to be legally sufficient to perfect a security interest. 1999 §§ 9-502(a); 9-516(b)(4), (5). A filing officer must refuse to accept an initial filing statement that omits addresses. 1999 § 9-520(a), 9-516(b). In other words, if a filing officer mistakenly files a financing statement that lacks the addresses of the parties, the filing is effective to perfect the security interest. On the other hand, if the filing officer does reject a financing statement due to a lack of addresses, perfection has not occurred. 1999 § 9-516(b). In general, see Comment 5 to 1999 § 9-516 which discusses the reasoning of the drafters regarding addresses of the parties.

e. Description of Collateral

The 1999 Code requires that the financing statement "indicate" the collateral covered by it. 1999 § 9-502(a)(3). As to the sufficiency of the identification (that is the description) of the collateral, the 1999 Code provides that a financing statement sufficiently describes the collateral if it provides a description that is sufficient for a security agreement. 1999 § 9-504(1). See Chapter 2, § 2c(2), for discussion of the requirement of description of collateral in a security agreement under the 1999

Code. Additionally, the 1999 Code authorizes the use of "super generic" descriptions on the financing statement only. Thus, the 1999 Code authorizes an indication that the financing statement covers "all assets" or "all personal property." 1999 § 9-504(2).

Example. Big Bank makes a business loan to Dean Dennis. Big Bank required Dean to grant it a security interest in Dean's equipment, inventory and accounts. Dean signed a security agreement to that effect. Big Bank filed a financing statement that described the collateral as "inventory and accounts;" equipment was inadvertently left out of the description. Although Big Bank has an attached security interest in Dean's equipment, the interest is unperfected because that collateral is not described in the financing statement.

f. Description of Real Estate

In general, the 1999 Code requires that to be sufficient a financing statement must include a description of real estate when the collateral is real-estate related. Such collateral includes "as-extracted" collateral which essentially is oil, gas, or other minerals or accounts arising out of the sale of such. For a complete definition of "as-extracted" collateral, see 1999 § 9-102(a)(6). A real estate description also is required for timber to be cut. Finally, if the financing statement is filed as a fixture filing and covers goods that are or are to become fixtures, a real estate description is required. The 1999 Code eliminates a 1972 Code requirement of a real estate description for a financing statement covering crops. As to the requirement of a real estate description for as-extracted collateral, timber to be cut, and fixtures, see 1999 § 9-502(b)(3).

The required description of real estate is adequate if it reasonably identifies what is described although a particular state enactment can require a description that would be sufficient to give constructive notice of a mortgage, i.e., a complete "legal" description. 1999 §§ 9-502(b)(3), 9-108.

As to collateral for which a description of real estate is required, the 1999 Code also requires the financing statement to satisfy the content requirements of any financing statement. See 1999 § 9-502(a), (b). Additionally, the financing statement must indicate that it covers the type of collateral; that it is to be filed in the real property records; and if the debtor does not have an interest of record in the real property, the financing statement must include the name of a record owner. 1999 § 9-502(b)(1), (2), (4). The 1999 Code also permits use of a mortgage in lieu of a financing statement if filed as a fixture filing or as a financing statement covering as-extracted collateral or timber to be cut. However, the mortgage must indicate the goods or accounts it covers and otherwise satisfy the requirements of a financing statement. 1999 § 9-502(c).

g. *Reference to Proceeds or Products of Collateral*

Under 1999 § 9-521(a), no reference to "proceeds" need be made on a financing statement. The reason is that, in most instances, perfection as to collateral under 1999 § 9-315(c) automatically perfects as to proceeds. See discussion in Chapter 4, § 8.

Where perfection as to proceeds is not automatic under the 1999 Code, perfection lapses after the twenty-first day after the security interest attaches to the proceeds, and a new filing is necessary to cover proceeds. 1999 § 9-315(d). Because the debtor's signature is not required on a financing statement under the 1999 Code, no signature of the debtor is required with regard to a financing statement filed when necessary to continue perfection in proceeds. See prior discussion in this chapter at § 3b.

The statutory form of prior 1972 § 9-402(3) contained the statement: "products of the collateral are also covered." Standard forms of financing statements contained a box making the above statement; all that need be done was to check such a "products" box. The 1999 statutory form of § 9-521, however, does not contain such a statement related to products of collateral.

Under the 1972 Code, the basic reason for claiming "products" was to follow a security interest into finished goods when a portion of a manufacturing process is being financed. Under 1972 § 9-315(1) (b), if a financing statement covering the original goods also covered the product into which the goods were manufactured, processed or assembled, the security interest continued in the product or mass. Under the 1999 Code, the security interest continues in the product or mass without regard to any mention of products on the financing statement. 1999 § 9-336.

h. Security Agreement or Reproduction as Financing Statement

Under 1972 § 9-402(1), a copy of the security agreement was sufficient as a financing statement if it contained the information required in a financing statement (as discussed in previous parts of this section) and was properly signed.

The 1999 Code has deleted any reference to filing

a security agreement in lieu of a financing statement. The drafters of the 1999 Code concluded that the 1972 provision was unnecessary and unwise. See Comment 4 to 1999 § 9-502. Even so, it would seem that if a security agreement satisfies all of the form requirements of a financing statement set forth at 1999 § 9-502, the security agreement could be filed and would effectively perfect the security interest.

§ 4.　Time of Filing

Article 9 has no provision, as existed in some pre-Code statutes, requiring a filing within a specified period of time after the debtor receives the collateral.

Although there is no prescribed time within which to file under the Code, delayed filing may result in subordination of the security interest to the claim of a third person. Moreover, if filing is delayed and is not made until within 90 days of bankruptcy of the debtor, the delayed filing might be set aside as a preferential transfer. See Chapter 8, § 5a.

It is not necessary to delay filing until a security agreement is made or until a security interest attaches. "A financing statement may be filed before a security agreement is made or a security interest otherwise attaches." 1999 § 9-502(d). However, where filing is premature, perfection does not take place until the security interest attaches. As to attachment of a security interest, see Chapter 3, § 1.

The time of filing is determined by 1999 § 9-516(a) which reads:

> "Except as otherwise provided in subsection (b), communication of a record to a filing office and tender of the filing fee or acceptance of the record by the filing office constitutes filing."

The 1999 Code specifies that filing does not occur with respect to a record that a filing office refuses to accept for reasons enumerated by the 1999 Code at 1999 § 9-516(b). A record that is communicated to the filing office with tender of the filing fee that the filing officer refuses to accept for any other reason is deemed effective or filed except against a purchaser of the collateral which gives value in reasonable reliance upon the absence of a filed record. 1999 § 9-516(d). Again, as to the effect of a mistake by the filing officer, see § 12b of this chapter.

§ 5.　Amendment to Financing Statement

Sometimes, an amendment to a financing statement may be filed. However, if any amendment adds collateral, it is effective as to the added collateral only from the filing date of the amendment. See 1999 § 9-512(c).

The 1999 Code permits secured parties of record to amend a filed financing statement without the need to obtain the debtor's signature. See Comment 3 to 1999 § 9-512. However, if the amendment adds collateral or adds a debtor, the debtor must have authorized the amendment or it will not be effective. 1999 §§ 9-509(a), 9-510(a). The 1999 Code also makes it clear that an amendment does not extend the period of effectiveness of a financing statement. 1999 § 9-512(b). A continuation statement should be filed when the effectiveness of a financing statement is to be extended. See § 7 of this chapter.

Normally, an amendment is filed when items or types of collateral are added which are not covered in the original financing statement. However, a security interest in additional units of a type of collateral already described in a filed financing statement can be created under an after-acquired property clause of a security agreement or a new security agreement; no amendment is necessary. See 1999 § 9-204(a), (b).

Example. A filed financing statement covers all radios as inventory in the hands of debtor retailer, under a security agreement covering "all present and future radios as inventory." Debtor who had been handling the X make of radio also takes on the Y make of radio. No new filing is necessary. But if debtor decides to handle refrigerators under financing by the secured party, a new security agreement is necessary and an amendment to the financing statement referring to refrigerators as inventory should be filed.

§ 6. Duration of Filing; Lapse

1999 § 9-515(a) flatly declares that a filed financing statement is good for five years. A special provision is added by the 1999 Code that applies to financing statements filed in connection with a public-finance transaction or a manufactured-home transaction which indicates such filings are effective for 30 years after the date of filing. 1999 § 9-515(b). Some exceptions to the five-year period exist, however:

(1) A filing stating that the debtor is a transmitting utility is good until a termination statement is filed. See 1999 § 9-515(f).

(2) A real estate mortgage effective as a fixture

filing is good until the mortgage is released or satisfied as of record or its effectiveness otherwise terminates as to the real estate. See 1999 § 9-515(g).

The effectiveness of a filed financing statement lapses at the expiration of the five-year or other period of duration, under 1999 § 9-515(c), unless a continuation statement is filed prior to the lapse. Upon such lapse, the security interest becomes unperfected. It is made clear that there is no lapse if the security interest is perfected in some other way (as where the secured party repossesses the collateral just before the end of the five-year period of the filing).

Under 1999 § 9-515(c), it is clear that if the security interest becomes unperfected upon lapse, it is deemed never to have been perfected "as against a purchaser of the collateral for value." Note that this provision of the 1999 Code does not apply to lien creditors. See Comment 3 to 1999 § 9-515.

Example. A and B both made nonpurchase-money advances against the same collateral, and both perfected security interests by filing. A, who filed first, is entitled to priority under 1999 § 9-322(a)(1). But if no continuation statement is filed, A's filing may lapse first. So long as B's interest remains perfected thereafter, B is entitled to priority over A's unperfected interest. This rule avoids a circular priority under some prior statutes, under which A was subordinate to the debtor's trustee in bankruptcy, with A retaining priority over B and B having priority over the trustee in bankruptcy.

§ 7.   Continuation Statement

When the period of a filing is about to expire, the secured party may extend the time of perfection by filing a continuation statement. The continuation statement may be filed within six months prior to the expiration of the five-year period of the original filing. 1999 § 9-515(d). A special provision is added by the 1999 Code that applies to financing statements filed in connection with public-finance transactions or manufactured-home transactions which indicates that a continuation statement may be filed only within six months before the expiration of the 30-year effective period specified in 1999 § 9-515(b).

The time within which to file a continuation statement is absolute; filing more than six months before the end of the five-year period of the original filing is ineffective. Moreover, if a filing has lapsed and no continuation statement is filed prior to lapse, a subsequently-filed continuation statement is ineffective. In that case, a new financing statement must be filed to revive perfection.

Example. Old Bank acquired a security interest in Diane Deem's collection of art to secure payment of a loan the bank made to her. The bank filed a proper financing statement. Five years and one month later, with the loan not fully paid, Diane filed bankruptcy. The trustee appointed in Diane's bankruptcy proceeding can avoid Old Bank's security interest because it is unperfected due to the fact the financing statement lapsed. If Old Bank had filed a continuation statement before the bankruptcy was filed, Old Bank's security interest would survive the bankruptcy. See Chapter 8, § 4.

Under the 1999 Code, a continuation statement need not be signed by the secured party or the debtor. This is consistent with regard to 1999 Code requirements related to the financing statement which do not require even the signature of the debtor on the initial financing statement.

Under the 1999 Code, the required contents of a continuation statement are set forth in the definition of "continuation statement." 1999 § 9-102(a)(27). The continuation statement must identify the initial financing statement and indicate that it is a continuation statement for the identified financing statement.

Upon timely filing of a continuation statement,

the effectiveness of the original filing is extended for five years after the last date to which the filing was effective. Succeeding continuation statements may be filed to extend the period for additional five-year periods. See 1999 § 9-515(e).

No continuation statement is necessary where the debtor is a transmitting utility, nor is it necessary where a real estate mortgage is effective as a fixture filing. See 1999 § 9-515(f), (g).

§ 8.   Assignment of Security Interest

1999 § 9-514 deals with filing when a security interest is assigned. In this regard, 1999 § 9-514(a) recognizes that an original financing statement may disclose an assignment by indicating the name and address of the assignee as the name and address of the secured party. In other words, this permits an initial filing in the name of the assignee as secured party.

Example.   Seller takes a security interest in widgets sold on credit to Buyer and at once assigns the security interest to Financer. Seller files a financing statement naming Financer as the secured party.

1999 § 9-514(b) provides that assignments of

security interests that occur after the initial filing may be filed. The filing reflecting an assignment is actually an amendment of the original financing statement and must identify the initial financing statement, provide the name of the assignor, and provide the name and mailing address of the assignee.

1999 § 9-514(c) make it clear that an assignment of a security interest in a fixture set forth in a mortgage effective as a fixture filing under 1999 § 9-502(c) may be made only by an assignment of the mortgage under the law governing mortgages.

Where an assignment of a security interest is disclosed in a filing or filed separately, the assignee becomes the secured party of record. See generally 1999 § 9-514.

It should be kept in mind that if a secured party assigns a perfected security interest, no filing under Article 9 is necessary to continue the perfected status of the security interest against creditors of and transferees from the original debtor. See 1999 § 9-310(c) and discussion in Chapter 4, § 9. Thus, filing of an assignment is optional under the 1999 Code.

§ 9.   Filings Reflecting Release of Collateral

Occasionally the debtor and secured party agree to release collateral from the security interest and wish to reflect that the release occurred by a filing in the UCC filing system. Under 1999 § 9-512, the release of collateral can be evidenced by filing an "amendment" of a financing statement. The required contents of an amendment releasing collateral under 1999 § 9-512 include that the initial financing statement be identified in the filed amendment.

Normally, an amendment reflecting release of collateral is used when there is a partial release of collateral. It may also be used when all the collateral is released but where the financing is to be continued, with other collateral substituted either at the time of release or at a later time. Upon substitution of other collateral, an amendment to the financing statement should be filed.

A statement of release should not be used when the secured transaction is ended. A termination statement should be used. See § 10 of this chapter which follows.

§ 10. Termination Statement

a. 1999 Code Provisions Related to Termination Statements for Collateral Other than Consumer Goods

The debtor in secured transactions in which the collateral is not consumer goods may demand a termination statement when the debtor believes the secured debt is paid and the secured transaction is at an end. Within twenty days after a secured party receives an authenticated demand from the debtor, the secured party must send to the debtor a termination statement or file the termination statement. 1999 § 9-513(c). That duty of the secured party arises upon such demand from the debtor if there is no obligation remaining and no commitment to make an advance in the future. 1999 § 9-513(c)(1). The obligation to provide or file the termination statement also arises after debtor demand if accounts or chattel paper were sold but as to which the account debtor or obligor has discharged their obligation; or when the goods were subject to a consignment to the debtor but are not in the debtor's possession; or the debtor did not authorize the filing of the initial financing statement. 1999 § 9-513(c)(2) - (4).

b. *1999 Code Provisions Related to Termination Statements for Consumer Goods Collateral*

When the collateral is consumer goods, the 1999 Code treats the termination statement differently. It requires the secured party to file a termination statement if there is no obligation remaining and no commitment to make an advance in the future or the debtor did not authorize the filing of the initial financing statement. 1999 § 9-513(a). Note that the duty is to file (not just provide) the termination statement and that the duty arises without the need for the debtor to make demand for a termination statement. On the other hand, if the secured party receives an authenticated demand from the consumer debtor, the secured party within twenty days must file a termination statement; in the absence of a demand, the secured party must file the termination statement within one month after there is no obligation remaining and no commitment to make another advance. 1999 § 9-513(b).

c. *Effect of Filing a Termination Statement*

If a termination statement is filed, the financing statement to which the termination statement relates ceases to be effective. If the debtor is a transmitting utility, the termination statement when filed also causes the effectiveness of the financing statement to lapse. 1999 § 9-513(d). See also 1999 §§ 9-519(g), 9-522(a), and 9-523(c).

d. Failure to File or Provide a Termination Statement

If the secured party fails to file a required termination statement in the case of consumer goods, or provide a required termination statement in other cases, the statement can be filed without the secured party's authorization. 1999 § 9-509(d)(2). Note that a secured party who improperly fails to file or provide a termination statement is liable for a $500 fine plus damages. 1999 § 9-625(b), (e)(4)

e. Form of Termination Statement

The 1999 Code treats a termination statement as an amendment to a financing statement. Thus, the termination statement must identify by file number the initial financing statement. It also must include either that it is a termination statement or that the filed financing statement is no longer effective. 1999 § 9-102(a)(79).

§ 11. Filing Where There Is Consignment or Lease

In certain instances, it may be desirable to file under Article 9 with respect to a lease or consignment of personal property, even where the lease or consignment is not intended to confer a security interest. For discussion of leases or consignments as secured transactions, see Chapter 2, § 5d and e.

1999 § 9-505 permits a filing covering consigned or leased goods. This permits a consignor or lessor to file a financing statement using the terms "consignor," "consignee," "lessor," "lessee" or the like, instead of the terms "debtor" and "secured party" used in 1999 § 9-502(a). The Article 9 provisions relating to the place of filing and the form of a financing statement apply as appropriate to such a financing statement. However, such a filing is not of itself a factor in determining whether or not the consignment or lease is intended as security. If it is determined that a consignment or lease is intended for security, a security interest of the consignor or lessor which attaches to the consigned or leased goods is perfected by such a filing.

This sets forth a special method of filing where a consignor or lessor desires to file without such a filing itself indicating an intent that the transaction be a secured transaction. In other words, a consignor or lessor may make a precautionary filing, although they may have good reason (such as a "tax" reason) to desire the transaction not be a secured transaction within Article 9. See Comment 2 to 1999 § 9-505. It should be noted that 1999 § 9-505 is an expanded version of former 1972 § 9-408. The 1999 Code provision "embrace[s] more generally other bailments and transactions" than just consignments and leases.

§ 12. Duties of Filing Officers

a. General Duties

Various duties of a filing officer (such as the Secretary of State, a county clerk or various employees) are spelled out in Article 9. Such duties are summarized as follows:

(1) Financing statements and other filings are to be marked with a file number and the date and hour of filing and are to be available for public inspection. They are to be indexed in the name of the debtor. 1999 § 9-519.

(2) A financing statement covering timber to be cut or minerals or the like (including oil and gas) or accounts resulting from the sale of minerals (including oil and gas) at the wellhead or minehead,

or a statement filed as a fixture filing is to be indexed under the name of the debtor and any owner of record shown on the statement in the same fashion as with respect to real estate mortgages. Optional language also specifies that the statement is to be filed for record. 1999 § 9-519(d), (e).

(3)   Rules are set forth as to removal and destruction of lapsed statements. 1999 § 9-522.

(4)   Procedures are set forth as to the marking and indexing of a filed statement of assignment, 1999 § 9-514, and a statement of release of collateral, 1999 § 9-512.

(5)   Procedures are set forth as to the handling of termination statements which are filed. 1999 § 9-513.

(6)   Schedules of various filing fees are set forth with respect to financing and other statements filed and increased fees are permitted where nonstandard forms are filed. 1999 § 9-525.

b. *Effect of Mistake of Filing Officer*

The 1999 Code specifies that communication of a record to a filing office and tender of the filing fee or acceptance of the record by the filing office constitutes filing. 1999 § 9-516(a). Thus, the filing secured party does not bear the risk of a filing officer's error, assuming the filing is "communicated" to the filing office with the filing fee or is otherwise accepted by the filing officer. Additionally, the 1999 Code specifically indicates that the failure of a filing officer to index or record correctly does not affect the effectiveness of the filed record. 1999 § 9-517.

The 1999 Code does provide an exclusive list of reasons for which a filing officer must reject the filing and further provides that refusal to accept for any of these reasons means filing does not occur. 1999 § 9-516(b). If the filing officer mistakenly rejects the filing for some other reason, the filing is effective except as against a purchaser of collateral which gives value in reasonable reliance upon the absence of the record from the files. 1999 § 9-516(d).

Example. A secured party filed a financing statement in proper form, accompanied by the proper filing fee, in the proper office. The filing officer erroneously indexed the statement in the records by showing the secured party as the debtor and the debtor as the secured party. The filing is effective.

c. *Information as to Filing*

A 1999 provision carries out a function of "notice filing" by specifying means of obtaining information from the filing officer as to a filing. 1999 § 9-523.

The filing officer shall, upon the request of the person who files, return to that person (normally the secured party) a copy of the statement filed bearing a notation of the file number and the date and hour of the filing. This applies to any statement filed. 1999 § 9-523(a), (b) and Comment 3.

A search procedure is set forth in 1999 § 9-523(c) - (e) which requires a filing officer upon request to issue to any person who has tendered the proper fee a certificate as to what filings have been made against any particular debtor and to furnish copies of such filed financing statements or statements of assignment at a fee based on the number of pages involved. This search procedure may be utilized by anyone, and is of obvious utility to prospective creditors and others who need to ascertain what collateral of a particular debtor is subject to a security interest.

A person who searches the files and discovers a filing may obtain further details of the transaction by utilizing (with the cooperation of the debtor) the procedure set forth in 1999 § 9-210. See discussion in Chapter 3, § 6.

CHAPTER 6

CHOICE OF LAW AND PERFECTION IN MULTIPLE STATE TRANSACTIONS

§ 1. General Principles

A general choice-of-law rule is set forth in both pre-revision and revised UCC Article 1.

In pre-revision Article 1, the general choice-of-law rule is pre-revision § 1-105, which is applicable to various commercial relationships arising under different Articles of the Uniform Commercial Code. That general rule applies to secured transactions, at least as between the debtor and the secured party. See Comment 2 to 1999 § 9-301. Under pre-revision § 1-105(1), the parties may by agreement determine the law that governs their relationship, so long as the transaction "bears a reasonable relation" to the jurisdiction the law of which is selected. Failing such specification of the law of a particular state by agreement, a court in a Code state may apply its own law (the Code) to transactions "bearing an appropriate relation" to the state. This suggests the likelihood that, in the absence of an agreement specifying the state whose law shall govern, a court will follow general conflict-of-laws principles and apply the law of the state having the most significant relationship with the transaction.

Governing law, as between the parties in the absence of agreement, will thus often be determined by the law of the place of contracting or the law of the place of performance. Moreover, the law of the place of location of the collateral will likely be applied where the question is the effect of some act affecting the collateral, such as the propriety of repossession or of sale of the collateral by the secured party following repossession.

Under revised § 1-301, the general choice-of-law rules set forth therein also apply to secured transactions, at least as between the debtor and the secured party. See again, Comment 2 to 1999 § 1-301. Under revised § 1-301, the parties also may by agreement determine the law that governs their relationship. Such an agreement is generally effective whether or not the transaction bears a relation to the law of the state selected by the parties' agreement. See revised § 1-301(c). However, if one of the parties is a consumer, such an agreement is effective only if the transaction has a reasonable relationship to the state whose law is selected, and the agreement may not deprive the consumer of the protection of consumer protection law. See revised § 1-301(e). In the absence of an agreement specifying the law of a particular state, the rights and obligations of the parties are determined by the law that would be selected by the application of the forum state's conflict-of-law principles. See revised § 1-301(d).

Although general choice-of-law principles in commercial transactions are governed by pre-revision § 1-105 and revised § 1-301, those provisions have but limited application with respect to secured transactions. The reason is that most secured transactions questions do not settle rights as between the debtor and the secured party, but instead litigate claims to the collateral as between the secured party and third persons. Choice-of-law problems where the rights of third persons are at issue frequently involve the perfection of the security interest in multiple state transactions, or what law governs the effect of perfection or non-perfection. See pre-revision § 1-105(2) and revised § 1-301(g)(8).

Accordingly, the balance of this chapter deals with the question of the state in which the security interest is to be perfected, in a multistate transaction. Such rules are set forth in 1999 §§ 9-301–9-307, 9-316, and 9-337. In addition, rules are set forth to determine the effect on perfection in one jurisdiction when the collateral is moved or the debtor moves to a second jurisdiction.

§ 2.   Where to Perfect a Security Interest in a Multiple State Transaction

Problems of conflict of laws or choice of law in commercial transactions should often be minimal where a uniform statute such as the Uniform Commercial Code is widely adopted. Nevertheless, a significant choice-of-law problem may arise where the question is in what state to file or take other action to perfect a security interest. Such a problem may also arise where collateral subject to a perfected security interest in one state is moved to another state, and no action is taken to perfect in the second state, or a debtor located in one state has granted a perfected security interest and later moves to another state and no action is taken to perfect in the second state.

The problems covered in the balance of this chapter might be summarized to some extent in the following hypothetical example:

Debtor, incorporated in State A with its chief executive office in State B, grants a security interest in goods located in State C to X who is located in

State D. Some of the goods are then sold by Debtor to Buyer and shipped to Buyer in State E. An account due from Buyer to Debtor arises, which is assigned by Debtor to Y in another secured transaction. Y is located in State F. Debtor keeps its account records in State G. Debtor then moves other goods to State H and there gives Z a security interest in those goods. What law governs the perfection of the various security interests?

These questions are answered by 1999 §§ 9-301–9-307, 9-316, and 9-337 which are concerned with the place to perfect the security interest and the effect of perfection or nonperfection. Other conflict-of-law problems not involving perfection are dealt with in pre-revision § 1-105 and revised § 1-301.

§ 3.   Governing Law Based on Location of Collateral

The 1999 Code provides that where the creditor has possession of the collateral, a so-called "possessory security interest," the law governing perfection and the priority of a security interest is the law of the jurisdiction in which the collateral is located. 1999 § 9-301(2). Since in most secured transactions the creditor does not take possession of the collateral, this rule will infrequently apply. A significantly different rule applies if the creditor is not in possession of the collateral. See subsequent discussion at § 4 of this chapter. It should be noted that the 1999 Code treats certificate-of-title collateral separately. See 1999 § 9-303 and later discussion in this chapter at § 7.

The law of the jurisdiction in which the collateral is located also governs perfection and priority issues if a fixture filing is involved or the collateral is timber to be cut. 1999 § 9-301(3). Similarly, if the collateral is "as-extracted" collateral, i.e., oil or gas and minerals [1999 § 9-102(a)(6)], the law of the jurisdiction in which the wellhead or minehead is located governs perfection and priority issues. 1999 § 9-301(4).

Because agricultural liens are within the scope of the 1999 UCC Article 9, a rule was necessary to designate which state in which the lien should be filed. While farm products are located in a particular state, the local law of that state governs the perfection and priority of agricultural liens in the farm products. 1999 § 9-302.

The 1999 Article 9 provides place-of-perfection rules regarding investment property. As to uncertificated securities, perfection of a security interest is governed by the law of the jurisdiction of the issuer. 1999 § 9-305(a)(2). See also § 8-110(d).

For certificated securities, the law of the state in which the certificate is located governs. 1999 § 9-305(a)(1). See also § 8-110(c). Other rules apply to all others forms of investment property. As to where to perfect a security interest in a security entitlement or a securities account, see 1999 § 9-305(a)(3); as to a commodity contract or commodity account, see 1999 § 9-305(a)(4). For general discussion of security interests in investment property, see Chapter 4, § 4b and Chapter 1, § 9a(3).

§ 4. Governing Law Based on Debtor's Location

a. General Rule under the 1999 Code

For most secured transactions under the 1999 Code, the law governing perfection and priority issues will be the law of the location of the debtor. Specifically, in most transactions in which the secured creditor is not in possession of the collateral, a so-called "nonpossessory" security interest, the law of the jurisdiction in which the debtor is located governs. 1999 § 9-301(1). The exceptions to the debtor-location rule for nonpossessory security interests include fixture filings, timber to be cut, and as-extracted collateral. 1999 § 9-301(3), (4). See discussion at § 5 of this chapter. Additionally, certificate-of-title collateral (1999 § 9-303), deposit accounts (1999 § 9-304), investment property (1999 § 9-305) and letter-of-credit rights (1999 § 9-306) are given separate treatment. As to investment property, see § 6 of this chapter; as to deposit accounts and letter-of-credit rights, see § 8 of this chapter.

The 1999 Code specifies where the debtor is located at 1999 § 9-307. If the debtor is an individual, the debtor is located at the debtor's principal residence. 1999 § 9-307(b)(1). Debtors that are "organizations" are treated differently. An "organization" includes a corporation, estate, trust, and a partnership. For a definition of "organization" see pre-revision § 1-201(28) and revised § 1-201(b)(25). A debtor that is an organization and has only one place of business is located at its place of business [1999 § 9-307(b)(2)]; if it has more than one place of business, it is located at its chief executive office [1999 § 9-307(b)(1)].

However, a "registered organization" that is organized under the law of a state is located in that state of organization. 1999 § 9-307(e). A "registered organization" usually means an organization organized under the law of a single state as to which the state must maintain a public record showing the organization to have been organized. 1999 § 9-102(a)(70). In other words, a registered organization typically is a debtor that is incorporated.

Example. Acme, Inc. obtains a loan from Big Bank and grants Big Bank a security interest in all of Acme, Inc.'s inventory and equipment. Big Bank is located in California; Acme, Inc. only does business in California. All of the collateral is located in California. However, Acme, Inc. is incorporated under the laws of Delaware. Big Bank must file its financing statement in Delaware.

The 1999 Code has separate debtor location rules for federally registered organizations which essentially require filings to be made in the District of Columbia. 1999 § 9-307(f), (h).

b. *Effect of Change of Location of Debtor Under the 1999 Code*

The 1999 Code deals with issues that arise when the debtor changes location to a new state after an initial filing. A security interest remains perfected until the *earliest* of the time perfection would have ceased under the law of the state in which perfection initially occurred; the expiration of four months after a change of the debtor's location to a new state; or the expiration of one year after a transfer of the collateral to a person that becomes a debtor and is located in another jurisdiction. 1999 § 9-316(a). Using the four-month portion of the above rule, this means the secured party must perfect, i.e., file a financing statement, in the new state within the four months after the change of the debtor's location to a new state; if the secured party fails to do so, the security interest becomes unperfected and is deemed never to have been perfected as against a purchaser of the collateral for value. 1999 § 9-316(b).

Example. Using the immediately prior example, assume Big Bank filed a financing statement in State B. Subsequently, Acme, Inc. reincorporated in State C. Big Bank must file a financing statement in State C within four months after the reorganization in State C to maintain perfection. If the debtor, Acme, Inc., sold collateral to a purchaser for value within the four-month period, or thereafter, the buyer would take free of the security interest if Big Bank fails to file in State C within the four-month period.

§ 5.   Collateral Related to Real Property

Some Article 9 collateral bears a close relation-ship to real property. Such collateral includes minerals, oil, gas and resulting accounts; timber to be cut; and fixtures. Additionally, agricultural liens relate to real property.

Under 1999 § 9-301(4), the place to perfect a security interest in minerals (including oil and gas) which attaches upon extraction is at the wellhead or minehead. The same rule governs with respect to accounts resulting from the sale of such items at the wellhead or minehead.

When the collateral is timber to be cut, the 1999 Code requires perfection in the state in which the timber is located. 1999 § 9-301(3)(B). The same rule applies to fixtures. 1999 § 9-301(3)(A).

The 1999 Code includes agricultural liens within its scope. It provides that while farm products are located within the state, that state governs perfection and priority issues related to the farm products. 1999 § 9-302.

§ 6.   Investment Property

The place of perfection as to investment property is governed by 1999 § 9-305. The law of the jurisdiction in which the debtor is located governs perfection of a security interest in investment property by filing as well as automatic perfection of a security interest in investment property created by a broker or securities intermediary. 1999 § 9-

305(c)(1),(2). Otherwise, while a security certificate is located in a jurisdiction, the law of that jurisdiction governs perfection of a security interest in the certificated security [1999 §9-305(a)(1)] and, as to uncertificated securities, the law of the issuer's jurisdiction as specified in § 8-110(d) governs perfection. 1999 § 9-305(a)(3). Other rules apply when the investment property is commodity-related. See 1999 § 9-305(a)(4), (b) and (c)(3).

For general discussion of security interests in investment property, see Chapter 4 § 4b and Chapter 1, § 9a(3).

§ 7. Collateral Where Certificate of Title Exists

The 1999 Code treats multi-state issues separately where a certificate of title exists. 1999 § 9-303 applies to goods covered by a certificate of title. The section applies even if there is no other relationship between the jurisdiction under whose certificate of title the goods are covered and the goods or the debtor. 1999 § 9-303(a). The lack of a requirement of a relationship between the state that issues a certificate of title to the goods or the debtor is in accord with cases that considered the matter under the 1972 Code. See Comment 2 to 1999 § 9-303.

1999 § 9-303 and related sections are summarized as follows:

(1) 1999 § 9-303(b) indicates when goods are covered by a certificate of title. Goods first become covered by a certificate of title when a valid application for the title and the application fee are delivered to the appropriate authority, such as a state department of motor vehicles. Such goods cease to be covered by a certificate of title in two situations. First, if the certificate of title ceases to be effective under the law of the issuing jurisdiction, the goods obviously are no longer subject to the certificate of title. The second situation arises when the goods become covered subsequently by a certificate of title issued by another jurisdiction. Unlike the former 1972 § 9-103(2)(b), the 1999 Code eliminates the concept of "surrender" as an event that results in the law of the state that issued the certificate of title not to apply. See Comment 3 to 1999 § 9-303. If, however, the certificate of title is surrendered to an appropriate authority in another state with a valid application and fee for a new title, the law of the state that originally issued the certificate of title ceases to apply.

(2) 1999 § 9-303(c) provides that the law of the jurisdiction under whose certificate of title the goods are covered governs perfection and priority issues

related to the security interest in the goods. That law governs until the goods cease to be covered by the certificate of title.

(3)   1999 § 9-316 deals with situations in which the goods cease to be covered by the certificate of title. The fact that the law of one jurisdiction ceases to apply under § 9-303(b) does not mean that a security interest perfected under that law becomes unperfected automatically. See Comment 4 to 1999 § 9-303. The gist of 1999 § 9-316(d) and (e) is that in most cases the security interest will remain perfected.

1999 § 9-316(d) indicates that a security interest in goods covered by a certificate of title, which is perfected by any method under the law of another jurisdiction when the goods become covered by a certificate of title in another state, remains perfected until the security interest would have become unperfected under the law of the other (former) jurisdiction had the goods not become so covered. However, 1999 § 9-316(e) provides an exception to this continuity of perfection rule.   The security interest becomes unperfected as against a purchaser of goods for value and is deemed never to have been perfected against such a purchaser if the applicable requirements for perfection are not satisfied before the earlier of either the time the security interest would have become unperfected under the law of the other jurisdiction had the goods not become covered by a certificate of title in the new state, <u>or</u> the expiration of four months after the goods have become so covered.

Example. Debtor grants a security interest to Big Bank on an automobile which is covered by a certificate of title issued by State A. Big Bank perfects the security interest by complying with State A's certificate-of-title statute. Debtor moves to State B and applies for a certificate of title in State B. One year later, Creditor obtains a judicial lien on the car. State A ceases to govern perfection once Debtor delivers the application and fee to State B authorities, at which time State B law governs. 1999 § 9-303(b). But, State B's 1999 § 9-316(d) provides that Big Bank's security interest remains perfected until it would become unperfected under State A's law had no certificate been issued by State B. Thus, Big Bank's security interest remains perfected and is senior to Creditor's judicial lien. See Comment 5 to 1999 § 9-316.

Example. Assume the same facts as described in the previous example except that after four months from the time Debtor applied for the State B certificate of title, Debtor sells the car to Buyer. Under these circumstances, Buyer takes free of Big

Bank's security interest. Lender did not reperfect within four months after the car became covered by the State B certificate of title. Thus, under 1999 § 9-316(e), Big Bank's security interest is deemed never to have been perfected against Buyer. See also 1999 § 9-317(b) and Comment 5 to 1999 § 9-316.

The 1999 Code adds one more section that must be considered when analyzing perfection and priority issues in certificate-of-title collateral when more than one state is involved. 1999 § 9-337 provides for priority for certain parties if, while a security interest in goods is perfected under the law of another state, a second state issues a certificate of title that does not show the goods are or may be subject to a security interest. Under these circumstances, a "nonprofessional buyer" takes free of the security interest if they gave value and did not know of the security interest. 1999 § 9-337(1). A "nonprofessional buyer" is a person not in the business of selling goods of the kind. Additionally, the security interest is subordinate to a conflicting security interest in the goods that attaches and is perfected after the issuance of a certificate and without the conflicting secured party's knowledge of the security interest. 1999 § 9-337(2).

§ 8. Multistate Perfection for Deposit Accounts and Letter-of-Credit Rights

The 1999 Code brings within its scope collateral in the form of some deposit accounts and letter-of-credit rights. 1999 §§ 9-109(a)(1), 9-102(a)(29), (51). See also discussion of these collateral types as falling within UCC Article 9's scope at Chapter 1, § 7e and Chapter 7, §§ 12 and 13. Secured transactions involving such collateral fell outside the scope of the 1972 Code. The inclusion of these types of collateral necessitated some new provisions applicable to multistate transactions in which deposit accounts and letter-of-credit rights serve as the collateral.

As to deposit accounts, the law of the bank's jurisdiction governs perfection and priority issues related to security interests in a deposit account maintained with that bank. 1999 § 9-304(a). The 1999 Code provides rules that determine a bank's jurisdiction [1999 § 9-304(b)] and rules that deal with situations in which the depositary bank changes jurisdictions. 1999 § 9-316(f).

As to letter-of-credit rights, the general rule is that the law of the jurisdiction of the party who issued the letter of credit governs perfection and priority issues related to security interests in letter-of-credit rights. The 1999 Code provides a rule that determines the jurisdiction of the issuer [1999 § 9-306(b)] and rules that deal with situations in which the issuer changes jurisdictions. 1999 § 9-316(f).

CHAPTER 7

PRIORITIES OF SECURED PARTIES AND OTHERS

§ 1. Introduction

As stated in the Comment to former 1972 § 9-101, the rules set out in Article 9 "are principally concerned with the limits of the secured party's protection against purchasers from and creditors of the debtor." See also Comment 1 to 1999 § 9-101 which states that "[f]or the most part [1999 Article 9] follows the general approach and retains much of the terminology of former [1972] Article 9."

The extent of protection of the secured party from claims of third persons with respect to the collateral depends in many instances on whether the security interest is perfected or not. The extent of such protection when the security interest is perfected is summarized in Comment 2 to 1999 § 9-308, which reads in part as follows:

"A perfected security interest may still be or become subordinate to other interests. ... However, in general, after perfection the secured party is protected against creditors and transferees of the debtor and, in particular, against any representative of creditors in insolvency proceedings instituted by or against the debtor."

While a perfected security interest is protected against most third-party claims, even an unperfected security interest has limited protection against certain third persons. See discussion in § 2b of this chapter.

The interests of third persons which compete with the interests of the secured party in the collateral fall into two basic classes: purchasers of the collateral and other creditors of the debtor. Note that if the debtor files bankruptcy, the trustee, as a representative of the debtor's creditors, also can become a competitor. Bankruptcy is considered in Chapter 8 of this Nutshell.

Such third-party competitors of the secured party for the collateral may be further broken down as follows:

(1) Buyers or transferees of the collateral

(2) Other secured parties.

(3) General or unsecured creditors.

(4) Creditors who have obtained a lien on the collateral by attachment, levy or the like.

(5) Representatives of creditors, such as an assignee for the benefit of creditors, a trustee in bankruptcy or a receiver, who have the status of lien creditors.

(6) Persons who have liens on the collateral by operation of law, such as the possessory lien of a repairman.

(7) Governmental units having liens by statute, such as the United States with a Federal tax lien.

For each priority dispute, there is a specific rule to determine which claimant has priority. Thus, it is important to identify carefully the basis of both parties' claims. Armed with that information, one is able to select the applicable priority rule. Otherwise stated, a single "first-in-time, first-in-right" rule will not suffice to resolve all priority disputes.

§ 2. Priority When Security Interest is Unperfected

a. *Priority Over Unperfected Security Interest*

The 1999 Code has a provision that sets forth the classes of persons who have priority with respect to collateral over the holder of an unperfected security interest. (It should be noted that the 1999 Code provisions also apply to unperfected agricultural liens. See § 14 of this chapter that discusses the priority of agricultural liens under the 1999 Code.)

The classes of persons who have priority with respect to the collateral over the holder of an unperfected security interest are listed in 1999 § 9-317, and include the following:

(1) Persons entitled to priority under 1999 § 9-322. That provision allows priority to particular kinds of secured parties with perfected security interests over a secured party with another perfected security interest. Thus, by implication an unperfected security interest is subordinate to another secured party's perfected security interest. This is clearly implied under 1999 §§ 9-317(a)(1) and 9-322(a)(1). In short, priority is given to the first to file or otherwise perfect a security interest under 1999 § 9-322(a)(1). See § 4a of this chapter.

(2) A person who becomes a lien creditor before the earlier of the time the security interest is perfected [1999 § 9-317(a)(2)(A)] or one of the conditions specified in 1999 § 9-203(b)(3) is met and a financing statement covering the collateral is filed. 1999 § 9-317(a)(2)(B). A security interest cannot be perfected until it has attached; the 1999 § 9-317(a)(2)(B) references to 1999 § 9-203(b)(3) are to requirements that must be satisfied in order

that the security interest can attach. Most important is § 9-203(b)(3)(A), which requires that the debtor authenticate a security interest.

Example 1.   Secured Party took a security interest in certain equipment, properly attaching and perfecting the security interest. A judgment creditor of the debtor subsequently had the sheriff levy on the equipment, thereby acquiring a lien. Under 1999 § 9-317(a)(2)(A), Secured Party has priority over the lien of the judgment creditor because the Secured Party perfected its security interest before the judgment creditor acquired its lien.

Example 2.   Debtor agreed to grant Secured Party a security interest in certain inventory to secure a loan Secured Party was contemplating making to Debtor in the future. The parties signed a security agreement. Secured Party filed a financing statement. A judgment creditor of the debtor subsequently had the sheriff levy on the inventory, thereby acquiring a lien. The next day, Secured Party agreed to and did make the loan to Debtor, at which time the security interest attached (value was given) and was perfected. Under 1999 § 9-317(a)(2)(B), Secured Party has priority over the lien of the judgment creditor because one of the 1999 § 9-203(b)(3) conditions was satisfied (the security agreement) and a financing statement was filed before the judicial lien was acquired. See Comment 4, 1999 § 9-317 for further explanation.

Note: A "lien creditor" is defined as "a creditor who has acquired a lien on the property involved by attachment, levy or the like and includes an assignee for the benefit of creditors from the time of assignment, and a trustee in bankruptcy from the date of the filing of the petition or a receiver in equity from the time of appointment." 1999 § 9-102(a)(52).

(3) Certain buyers of tangible chattel paper, tangible documents, goods, instruments or a security certificate. This excludes the secured party as a buyer. The buyer has to give value and receive delivery of the collateral *without knowledge of the security interest* and before it is perfected. See1999 § 9-317(b). The 1999 Code also gives lessees priority that receive delivery of collateral subject to an unperfected security interest. 1999 § 9-317(c).

(4) Certain licensees of a general intangible or a buyer of accounts, general intangibles, electronic chattel paper, and investment property other than certificated securities. 1999 § 9-317(d). The licensee or buyer must give value *without knowledge of the security interest* and before it is perfected.

b. *Priority of Unperfected Security Interest Over Others*

By a converse reading of 1999 § 9-317, which is discussed immediately above, certain classes of third-person claimants have rights in the collateral subordinate even to an unperfected security interest. These include:

(1) General creditors of the debtor who have no liens on the collateral. However, it should be noted that a representative of general creditors (such as an assignee for the benefit of creditors, a trustee in bankruptcy, or a receiver) would have priority as a lien creditor under 1999 §§ 9-317(a)(2) and 9-102(a)(52).

(2) Certain buyers of tangible chattel paper, tangible documents, goods, instruments, or a security certificate who have knowledge of the security interest. 1999 § 9-317(b). As to lessees who take delivery with knowledge of an unperfected security interest, the lessee also takes subject to the security interest under the 1999 Code. 1999 § 9-317(c).

(3) Certain transferees (licensees and buyers) of accounts and general intangibles (and some other forms of collateral) who have knowledge of the security interest. See 1999 § 9-317(d).

(4) A secured party with an unperfected security interest also has rights superior to those of a second secured party with an unperfected security interest whose security interest attaches at a time later than when the first security interest attaches. See1999 § 9-322(a)(3).

c. Grace Period for Filing Purchase-Money Security Interest

Ordinarily when a filing is made after the time the security interest attaches while otherwise unperfected, the filing is effective to perfect the security interest only from the time it is made. See 1999 §§ 9-308(a), 9-516(a). In other words, there is ordinarily no relation back of a filing, or grace period within which a filing may be made, except as set forth below. See Comment 5 to 1972 § 9-301 and, c.f., Comment 8 to 1999 § 9-317.

A limited 20-day grace period is given in 1999 § 9-317(e) with respect to a *purchase-money security interest*. The period is 20 days after the debtor receives possession of the collateral, and this can cut off the interests only of intervening buyers, lessees, or lien creditors. 1999 § 9-317(e).

Example 1. Debtor gives Secured Party a purchase-money security interest in widgets which are delivered to Debtor on April 1. Secured Party files on April 10. The filing within 20 days is sufficient to give Secured Party priority over Creditor who obtained a judgment lien on the collateral on April 3.

Example 2. Debtor gives Secured Party a non-purchase-money security interest in widgets on April 1. Secured Party files on April 10. The filing is ineffective as to any of the conflicting claimants described in 1999 § 9-317(a) who obtained their rights in the collateral prior to the filing.

Note the similar 20-day grace period under 1999 § 9-324(a) for protection of the purchase-money secured party against another secured party (except as to inventory collateral). See § 4b of this chapter.

§ 3.   Priority When Collateral Is Sold or Transferred

a. *Unauthorized Sale*

"Except where otherwise provided in this article and in Section 2-403(2): ... a security interest or agricultural lien continues in collateral notwith-standing sale, lease, license, exchange, or other disposition thereof unless the secured party authorized the disposition free of the security interest or agricultural lien...." 1999 § 9-315(a)(1). Thus, if the debtor makes an unauthorized sale of the collateral, the security interest continues in the collateral in the hands of the buyer, unless the buyer takes free of the security interest under some other provision of Article 9. The security interest also attaches to the proceeds of the sale. 1999 § 9-315(a)(2). The secured party may claim both the original collateral and proceeds, but may of course have only one satisfaction. See Comment 3 to 1999 § 9-315.

It should be noted that 1999 § 9-401 recognizes that a debtor's equity in the collateral may be sold or transferred involuntarily, whether or not the secured party consents, but such transfer is subject to the security interest. See discussion in Chapter 3, § 9.

The above does not mean that all buyers of the collateral take subject to the security interest when the collateral is sold without the consent of the secured party. Certain classes of buyers take free of even a perfected security interest and additional classes take free of an unperfected security interest.

Buyers or other transferees who take the collateral free of even a perfected security interest, in the event of an unauthorized sale, include the following:

(1) A buyer in the ordinary course of business. 1999 § 9-320(a).

(2) A consumer-buyer of consumer goods from another consumer, where the secured party has perfected without filing. 1999 § 9-320(b).

(3) A buyer of the collateral with respect to certain future advances made after sale of the collateral. 1999 § 9-323(c)-(f).

(4) Certain purchasers of chattel paper and instruments who give new value and take possession. 1999 § 9-330.

(5) Persons who have the status of holder in due course or like status with respect to a negotiable instrument, a negotiable document of title or a security. 1999 § 9-331.

The above group of buyers and transferees also takes free of an unperfected security interest. See discussion of each such group later in this section of the chapter.

Certain additional classes of buyers take free of an unperfected security interest. For discussion, see § 2a of this chapter.

b. Sale With Consent of Secured Party

1999 § 9-315(a)(1) makes it clear that a security interest in collateral is lost where its sale or disposition is *authorized by the secured party* in the security agreement or otherwise. Obviously, a secured party may expressly authorize the sale of the collateral by the debtor. The sale may also be impliedly authorized through conduct on the part of the secured party, as where the debtor repeatedly on prior occasions made sales of the same kind of collateral which were known to the secured party and to which no objection was voiced. In some instances, the secured party may expressly or by conduct be deemed to have waived a term in the security agreement which prohibits sale by the debtor. Consent to a sale may also be implied through the common-law concepts of waiver and estoppel. See pre-revision § 1-103 and revised § 1-103(b).

c. Buyer in Ordinary Course of Business

(1) General Rule

A buyer in ordinary course of business "takes free of a security interest created by the buyer's seller, even though the security interest is perfected and even though the buyer knows of its existence." 1999

§ 9-320(a). However, this rule does not apply to a person buying farm products from a person engaged in farming operations. See § 3c(2) of this chapter.

A lengthy definition of the term "buyer in ordinary course of business" is set forth in pre-revision § 1-201(9) and revised § 1-201(b)(9). That definition should be read with 1999 § 9-320(a) in determining whether a particular buyer of collateral takes free of a perfected security interest. The following is a summary of different applications or nonapplications of the "buyer in ordinary course of business" rule:

(a)   The rule applies whether the security interest is perfected or unperfected. Note that where the security interest is unperfected, other classes of buyers also take free of the security interest under 1999 § 9-317(b), (c). See § 2 of this chapter.

(b)   The rule applies where the sale is unauthorized by the secured party. If the secured party has authorized the sale in the security agreement or otherwise, the buyer takes free of the security interest without regard to the limitations of 1999 § 9-320(a). Note that 1999 § 9-315(a)(1) permits a buyer to take free of a security interest where the sale is authorized by the secured party. See § 3b of this chapter.

(c)   The definition of "buyer in ordinary course of business" in pre-revision § 1-201(9) and revised § 1-201(b)(9) is restricted to a buyer (except a pawnbroker) "from a person in the business of selling goods of that kind." Thus, the rule of 1999 § 9-320(a) *applies primarily to a buyer of inventory.*

Example 1. A buyer of a car from an automobile dealer is a buyer in ordinary course of business and takes free of a security interest given by the dealer. The same rule may apply where one dealer buys a car from another dealer, since dealers frequently sell cars to other dealers.

Example 2. A buyer of goods which are not inventory is not ordinarily regarded as a buyer in ordinary course of business and thus takes subject to a perfected security interest created by the seller of the goods. This principle has been applied to a buyer of an automobile used as equipment by a car repair garage which was not an auto dealer. It has also been applied where the seller is a company in the business of renting cars, even though the company from time to time replaces its stock of cars available for rental and sells the replaced cars. There is a contrary case authority, holding that a car-leasing company which from time to time sells leased cars is in the business of selling cars and can confer title free of a security interest on a buyer in ordinary course of business.

(d)   A buyer in ordinary course of business is one who buys "in good faith, without knowledge that the sale violates the rights of another person in the goods." Pre-revision § 1-201(9) and revised § 1-201(b)(9). This means that a buyer takes free of the security interest if they merely know that there is a security interest which covers the goods; but they take subject to that interest if they know, in addition, that the sale is in violation of some term in the security agreement not waived by the words or conduct of the secured party.

Example 3. Retailer gave a security interest in inventory to manufacturer. The security agreement prohibited sales by Retailer to other persons in the retail business who might buy for the purpose of selling the items at discount. Buyer, another retailer, knew of this prohibition in the security agreement, but nonetheless bought some of the inventory covered by the security agreement from Retailer. Buyer takes subject to the security interest.

(e)   A buyer in ordinary course of business may buy for cash or by exchange of other property (e.g., by a trade-in) or on secured or unsecured credit, and may receive goods or documents of title under a pre-existing contract for sale. However, there can be no buyer in ordinary course of business where there is a transfer in bulk (as where a business is sold to another) or where there is a transfer as security for or in total or partial satisfaction of a money debt. See pre-revision § 1-201(9) and revised § 1-201(b)(9). In other words, a person taking a security interest is not a buyer in ordinary course of business. Also, a person who takes collateral in satisfaction of a debt is not a buyer in ordinary course of business.

Example 4. Seller-Dealer owed money to Contractor arising from prior transactions between the two parties. Seller-Dealer transferred a truck to Contractor in satisfaction of the debt. Contractor is not a buyer in ordinary course of business and takes the truck subject to a security interest perfected by Creditor. But where Contractor purchased a truck from Seller-Dealer partly for cash, partly through trade-in of an older truck and partly by cancellation of a debt owed Contractor by Seller-Dealer, Contractor is a buyer in ordinary course of business.

Note: Although a person taking a security interest is not a buyer in ordinary course of business, a person taking a security interest in collateral purchased by a buyer in ordinary course of business takes free of any other security interest which is cut off by the buyer in ordinary course of business.

(f)   A buyer in ordinary course of business

takes free of a security interest only if it was *created by their seller*. 1999 § 9-320(a).

Example 5. A bought a car from dealer X and gave a security interest in the car to Bank M. Without authority from M, A sold the car to dealer Y. Dealer Y then sold the car to B who gave a security interest to Bank N. Although B is a buyer in ordinary course of business, B (and N) take subject to the security interest of M since that had not been created by Y who sold the car to B, but had been created by an earlier owner of the car, A.

(g)   A buyer of minerals or the like (including oil and gas) at the wellhead or minehead may be considered a buyer in ordinary course of business. See pre-revision § 1-201(9) and revised § 1-201(b)(9).

(2) Buyer of Farm Products

An exception to the rule permitting a buyer in ordinary course of business to take free of a security interest created by their seller is made where the buyer is "a person buying farm products from a person engaged in farming operations." 1999 § 9-320(a).

Although this special rule has been criticized in a number of quarters, it existed in the 1972 Code and has been retained in the1999 Code. The rule has been applied where a farmer or rancher obtains a loan and grants a security interest in crops or livestock. Under 1999 § 9-320(a), the secured party in such a case may follow the security interest into the hands of a buyer of the crops, such as a grain elevator or food processor, or into the hands of a buyer of livestock.

The "farm products" exception usually applies only where the secured party has a perfected security interest. If the secured party has an unperfected security interest, the buyer may take free of the security interest under 1999 § 9-317(b). The "farm products" exception does not apply where the farmer processes the crop into something else and then sells the resulting product.

Example 1. A farmer gave a security interest in a crop of peanuts to an agency of the United States government which filed a financing statement. The farmer then sold the crop to a company that buys and sells farm products. The company took the crop subject to the security interest and was liable to the United States for conversion when it resold the crop.

Example 2. A farmer gave a security interest in a crop of cotton to an agency of the United States government which filed a financing statement. The farmer ginned the cotton in their own ginning mill and then sold the product. Since the cotton had ceased to be "farm products" after ginning, the buyer took free of the security interest.

In response to criticism of the farm products exception, Congress enacted preemptive legislation as a part of the Food Security Act of 1985. See 7 U.S.C.A. § 1631. This federal statute provides that, regardless of 1999 § 9-320(a), farm product buyers take free of security interests in farm products created by their seller. However, the statute does set forth two exceptions under which the buyer takes subject to the security interest.

The first exception is a "prenotification" exception under which the buyer will take subject to the perfected security interest if within one year before the sale the buyer has received written notice of the security interest from either the secured party or the debtor. The federal statute contemplates that the debtor will provide the secured party with a list of buyers to whom to give notice. In order to "encourage" the debtor to do so, the statute provides that if the farmer-debtor sells farm products to someone not on the list, the debtor is subject to civil penalty as set forth in the statute.

The second exception arises if a state has established a special "central filing system." The federal legislation in effect encourages states to do so. If a state has established such a central filing system, the secured creditor must file an "effective financing statement" in this central filing system, a system that is established and maintained separately from a UCC Article 9 central filing system. Farm product buyers also would be required to register with the same central filing office. That office would then compile a master list organized by type of farm product and by the county where each product is produced. The filing office then will distribute the master list of security interests to registered buyers. Thus, theoretically a buyer would receive notice of a security interest in a particular seller's farm products and would take subject to the security interest should they choose to buy from that farmer-seller.

d. Buyer Where Purchase-Money Security Interest Is Automatically Perfected in Consumer Goods

"...[A] buyer of goods from a person who used or bought the goods for use primarily for personal, family, or household purposes takes free of a security interest, even if perfected, if the buyer buys ... without knowledge of the security interest ... for value ... primarily for the buyer's personal, family, or household purposes ... and before the filing of a financing statement covering the goods." 1999 § 9-320(b).

Under 1999 § 9-309(1), no filing is required to perfect a purchase-money security interest in consumer goods except motor vehicles required to be registered and where a fixture filing is necessary to obtain priority over conflicting interests in fixtures under 1999 § 9-334. Even though the security interest is perfected automatically upon attachment in such case, a buyer meeting the conditions of 1999 § 9-320(b) takes free of the perfected security interest. But if the purchase-money secured party files, any buyer takes the consumer goods subject to the security interest.

To come within this provision, a buyer must buy (a) without knowledge of the security interest, (b) for value, and (c) for "consumer" purposes. In other words, the rule applies only to a consumer buying consumer goods from another consumer. The purchase must be made before a financing statement is filed.

For discussion of 1999 § 9-309(l) permitting perfection automatically upon attachment of a purchase-money security interest in consumer goods, see Chapter 4, § 2a.

Example 1. Jones bought a deep freeze for home use from Appliance Company and gave Appliance a purchase-money security interest in the deep freeze for the unpaid price. Appliance did not file a financing statement. Six months later, Jones sold the deep freeze to a next door neighbor, Smith, who bought it for home use. Although Appliance has a perfected security interest, the sale is free of that interest if Smith bought for value and without knowledge of the security interest. But if Appliance had filed, Smith's purchase would be subject to the security interest.

Example 2. Jones bought a deep freeze for home use from Appliance Company and gave Appliance a purchase-money security interest in the deep freeze for the unpaid price. Appliance did not file a financing statement. Six months later, Jones traded in the deep freeze to Frosty, another dealer in deep freezes, for a more expensive model. Even though Appliance did not file, it has a security interest superior to the rights of Frosty, since the latter did not buy for personal, family or household purposes.

e. Where Future Advances Are Made After Sale of the Collateral

Under 1999 § 9-323(d), (f), a buyer, even though they may otherwise purchase collateral subject to a security interest, takes free of that security interest "to the extent that it secures advances made after the earlier of ... the time the secured party acquires knowledge of the buyer's purchase, or ... 45 days after the purchase." This rule does not apply if the advance is made pursuant to a commitment entered into without knowledge of the purchase and before the expiration of the 45-day period. See 1999 § 9-323(e), (g).

Example 1. Jones, a retailer, gave Secured Party a security interest in inventory under a security agreement permitting Secured Party at its option to make future advances to enable Jones to acquire additional inventory. Secured Party promptly filed a financing statement. More than six months later, on March 1, Jones sold the business to Smith without the knowledge or consent of Secured Party. On April 1, Jones borrowed $10,000 from Secured Party purportedly to buy more inventory. On May 1, Jones borrowed another $10,000 on a like representation. Secured Party learned of the sale to Smith on June 1. Under 1999 § 9-323(d), Secured Party has a security interest in the inventory transferred from Jones to Smith which is good against Smith to the extent of any indebtedness of Jones prior to March 1 and also to the extent of the April 1 advance. But Secured Party's interest is not good against Smith as respects the May 1 advance, which was made more than 45 days after the sale to Smith.

Note: In the above example, if Secured Party on April 1 (less than 45 days after the sale) had made a binding commitment to advance $10,000 on May 1, Secured Party's interest would have been good against Smith as respects the $10,000 advanced on May 1 to Jones.

Example 2. Debtor S gave lender L a purchase-money security interest in a boat in April, 2006, which security interest was promptly perfected. In August, 2006, S sold the boat to R. In June, 2007, S borrowed additional sums from L, part of which was used to pay off the balance due on the former loan and part of which was used for other purposes. Since the additional borrowing was more than 45 days after the sale of the boat, the additional sum loaned is a future advance. Moreover, the entire new loan is a future advance if the former loan is extinguished. The result is that R takes the boat free of the security interest to the extent that it secures such future advances.

f. Purchaser of Chattel Paper or Instrument

When a security interest is taken in inventory, proceeds of the sale of inventory are also subject to the security interest. In some instances, the proceeds may consist of chattel paper or instruments. For example, a secured party may finance an inventory of automobiles or appliances in the hands of a dealer. A credit buyer of a car or appliance from the dealer may sign a promissory note and grant a security interest by way of a security agreement (chattel paper) for the unpaid price, or they may just sign a promissory note (instrument) for the price.

A security interest in chattel paper may be perfected either by the secured party taking possession, 1999 §§ 9-310 (b)(6) and 9-313(a), or by filing, 1999 § 9-312(a). It may also be perfected where the chattel paper is proceeds if the security interest in the inventory giving rise to the proceeds is perfected. See 1999 § 9-315(c)-(e).

Although it is possible to perfect a security interest in an instrument by filing under the 1999 Code [1999 § 9-312(a)], normally perfection will still occur by taking possession. The security interest may be temporarily perfected for not over 20 days without possession under 1999 § 9-312(e) and (f). It may also be perfected where the instrument is proceeds if the security interest in the inventory giving rise to the proceeds is perfected, 1999 § 9-315(c)-(e).

Where a secured party has a perfected security interest in chattel paper or an instrument without being in possession, the debtor who remains in possession may transfer the chattel paper or instrument to a third person who takes possession. That third person then has an interest as a purchaser (or a security interest perfected through possession) in conflict with the nonpossessory but perfected interest of the secured party. 1999 § 9-330 sets forth circumstances under which the purchaser of chattel paper or an instrument may take possession and acquire rights superior to those of the secured party with the nonpossessory perfected security interest.

Under 1999 § 9-330 as to chattel paper, a purchaser of it has priority over a security interest in it which is claimed merely as proceeds of inventory subject to a security interest if the purchaser, in good faith and in the ordinary course of the purchaser's business, gives new value and takes possession or obtains control of the chattel paper and the paper does not indicate it has been assigned to one other than the purchaser. 1999 § 9-330(a); see also, 1999 § 9-105. As to any other security interest in the chattel paper, the purchaser takes free of the security interest if they gave value and took possession or control of the paper in good faith and in the ordinary course of the purchaser's business and if the purchaser had no knowledge that the purchaser was violating the rights of a secured party. 1999 § 9-330(b).

Example.   Dealer gave financer A a security interest in its inventory of automobiles and in proceeds of the sale of inventory which A perfected. Dealer sold a car to Buyer who executed a security agreement (chattel paper) on the car for the unpaid purchase price. Dealer then physically transferred the security agreement to financer B which acquired the paper for value, and which regularly acquired such security agreements representing sales of automobiles from Dealer. Even though B knew that A was financing Dealer's acquisition of inventory, B has priority as to Buyer's security agreement over the claim of A to that agreement as proceeds of inventory. The only claim of A is to the subsequent proceeds arising from the sale by Dealer of the chattel paper to B.

As to instruments, 1999 § 9-330(d) gives a purchaser of an instrument priority over a security interest in the instrument perfected by a method other than possession. To obtain this priority, the purchaser must give value and take possession in good faith and without knowledge that the purchaser is violating the rights of the secured party.

g. Purchaser of Instrument or Document With Holder in Due Course or Like Status

Under 1999 § 9-331, a purchaser of paper which is negotiable, including negotiable instruments, negotiable documents and investment securities, who has the status of holder in due course (or analogous status with respect to a negotiable document or an investment security), has priority over an earlier security interest even though perfected. Filing under Article 9 does not constitute notice of such earlier security interest to any holder or purchaser.

Example. Secured Party filed a financing statement covering all accounts due or to become due Debtor. Account Debtor, who owed money to Debtor on an account, mailed a check to Debtor in payment. Debtor indorsed and delivered the check to Creditor to whom Debtor also owed money. If Creditor takes the check as a holder in due course under Article 3 of the Code (which includes taking without knowledge of Secured Party's interest), Creditor has priority over Secured Party with respect to the check. The filing gave no notice of the security interest to Creditor.

§ 4.   Priority Between Secured Parties

a. The "First-to-File-or-Perfect" Rule

(1) Generally

1999 §§ 9-322 through 934 set forth a number of rules governing priority between conflicting security interests in the same collateral. Special rules exist with respect to conflicting security interests in inventory where one of the interests is a purchase-money interest, and conflicting interests in other collateral where one of the interests is a purchase-money interest. See 1999 § 9-324, discussed in § 4b of this chapter.

The general rule governing priority between perfected security interests in the same collateral (in the absence of a special rule) is stated in 1999 § 9-322(a)(1) as follows:

> "Conflicting perfected security interests ... rank according to priority in time of filing or perfection. Priority dates from the earlier of the time a filing covering the collateral is first made or the security interest ... is first perfected, if there is no period thereafter when there is neither filing nor perfection."

This rule also applies to agricultural liens under the 1999 provision. As to agricultural lien priority, see also 1999 § 9-322(a)(2) and (3). The priority of agricultural liens under the 1999 Code is also discussed at § 14 of this chapter.

This rule gives special effect to filing, which may take place even before the security interest attaches (and accordingly before it is perfected). The rule also recognizes that perfection may take place in one way and then in another way [as where the secured party is in possession, then releases the collateral to the debtor but has temporary perfection under 1999 § 9-312(e) or (f), and then files before the end of the period of temporary perfection]. If perfection remains continuous, the time of initial perfection is determinative.

Note that if the conflicting security interests are both unperfected, the first to attach has priority. See 1999 § 9-322(a)(3).

Application of the general "priority" rules between conflicting security interests is illustrated by the following examples. See also Comment 4 to 1999 § 9-322:

Example 1. Old Bank files against Debtor on July 1. New Bank files against Debtor on August 1. New Bank makes a nonpurchase-money advance against certain collateral on October 1 before Old Bank has made an advance. Old Bank has priority even though New Bank's advance was made earlier and its security interest was perfected when made. It makes no difference whether or not Old Bank knew of New Bank's interest when it made its advance.

Example 2. Old Bank and New Bank make nonpurchase-money advances against the same collateral. The collateral is in Debtor's possession and neither interest is perfected when the second advance is made. Whichever secured party first perfects its interest (by taking possession of the collateral or by filing) takes priority and it makes no difference whether or not it knows of the other interest at the time it perfects its own.

Example 3. Old Bank has a temporarily perfected (21 day) security interest, unfiled, in a negotiable document in Debtor's possession under 1999 § 9-312(e) or (f). On the fifth day, New Bank files and thus perfects a security interest in the same document. On the tenth day, Old Bank files. Old Bank has priority, whether or not it knows of New Bank's interest when it files, because it perfected first and has maintained continuous perfection or filing.

(2) Where Future Advances Are Made

If future advances are made while a security interest is perfected by filing or the taking of possession, the security interest with priority under the "first to file or perfect" rule of 1999 § 9-323(a) has the same priority with respect to the future advances. See 1999 § 9-323(a) and Comment 3 to 1999 § 9-323.

Example. On February 1 Old Bank makes an advance against machinery in Debtor's possession and files its financing statement. On March 1 New Bank makes an advance against the same machinery and files its financing statement. On April 1 Old Bank makes a further advance, under the original security agreement, against the same machinery (which is covered by the original financing statement and thus perfected when made). Old Bank has priority over New Bank both as to the February 1 and as to the April 1 advance and it makes no difference whether or not Old Bank knows of New Bank's intervening advance when it makes its second advance. Old Bank wins, as to the April 1 advance, because it first filed even though New Bank's interest attached, and indeed was perfected, before the April 1 advance. The same rule would apply if either Old Bank or New Bank had perfected through possession.   The same result would be reached even though Old Bank's April 1 advance was not under the original security agreement but was under a new security agreement under Old Bank's same financing statement or during the continuation of Old Bank's possession. See Comment 3 to 1999 § 9-323.

b. *Where There Is Purchase-Money Security Interest*

(1) Noninventory Collateral

"...[A] perfected purchase-money security interest in goods other than inventory ... has priority over a conflicting security interest in the same goods, and, ... a perfected security interest in its identifiable proceeds also has priority, if the purchase-money security interest is perfected when the debtor receives possession of the collateral or within 20 days thereafter." 1999 § 9-324(a). For discussion of priority as to proceeds, see § 4d of this chapter.

1999 § 9-324(a) is summarized as follows:

(a) The section states a general rule applicable to all kinds of collateral except inventory and gives the holder of a purchase-money security interest priority in such collateral as equipment, if the purchase-money security interest is perfected when the debtor receives possession of the collateral or within 20 days thereafter. This means that the purchase-money secured party either has filed a financing statement before the end of 20 days or has a temporarily perfected security interest in goods covered by documents under 1999 § 9-312(e) or (f), which is continued in a perfected status before the expiration of the 20-day period there specified. There is no requirement that the purchase-money secured party be without notice or knowledge of the other security interest; they take priority although they know of the other interest or that interest has been filed.

(b) The equivalent 1972 Code provision allowed a 10-day grace period for filing by the purchase-money secured party after the debtor receives possession of the collateral for protection against any other secured party. A number of states under the 1972 Code extended the period to 20 days or some other period, by non-uniform amendment to 1972 § 9-312(4). The 1999 Code provides for a 20-day period as well. 1999 § 9-324(a). Note the 20-day grace period under 1999 § 9-317(e) for protection of the purchase-money secured party against a lien creditor. See § 2c of this chapter.

Example 1. On February 1 Old Bank makes advances to X under a security agreement which covers "all the machinery in X's plant" and contains an after-acquired property clause. Old Bank promptly files a financing statement. On March 1 X acquires a new machine, New Bank makes an advance against it and files a financing statement. On April 1 Old Bank, under the original security agreement, makes an advance against the machine acquired March 1. If New Bank's advance creates a purchase-money security interest, they have priority (provided they filed before X received possession of the machine or within 20 days). If New Bank's advance, although they gave new value, did not create a purchase-money interest, Old Bank has priority as to both advances by virtue of their priority in filing, although the parties perfected simultaneously on March 1 as to the new machine.

(c)   Where a purchase-money secured party fails to file or perfect before the debtor receives possession of the collateral or within 20 days thereafter, priority is governed by the "first to file or perfect" rule of 1999 § 9-322(a), and not by 1999 § 9-324(a). For discussion of the "first to file or perfect" rule, see § 4a of this chapter.

(d)   The 1999 Code contains a provision that determines priority between two conflicting purchase-money security interests. 1999 § 9-324(g). It grants priority to a purchase-money security interest created in favor of a seller over a purchase-money security interest held by a third-party lender. Otherwise, the first-to-file-or-perfect rule of 1999 § 9-322(a) applies.

(e)   It should be noted that the 1999 Code has some special provisions regarding purchase-money security interest priority in livestock [1999 § 9-324(d), (e)] and software [1999 § 9-324(f)].

(2) Inventory Collateral

Where the collateral is inventory and there are conflicting security interests, under the 1999 Code the holder of a purchase-money interest is favored over other secured parties, but they must perfect their interest before the debtor receives the inventory and must also take certain other steps.

Under 1999 § 9-324(b), the purchase-money secured party with an interest in inventory has priority over a conflicting security interest in the same inventory if:

(a)   The purchase-money security interest is perfected at the time the debtor receives possession of the inventory. In other words, there is no 1999 Code 20-day grace period as exists with respect to other kinds of collateral.

(b)   The purchase-money secured party gives

notification to the holder of the conflicting security interest if the holder had filed a financing statement covering the same types of inventory before the date of the filing made by the purchase-money secured party (or before the beginning of the period of temporary perfection under 1999 § 9-312(f). Under the 1999 Code, the notice must be an "authenticated notification" which includes both a signed, written notice or an electronic notice with an encrypted signature.

(c)   The holder of the conflicting security interest receives the notification within five years before the debtor receives possession of the inventory.

(d)   The notification states that the person giving the notice has or expects to acquire a purchase-money security interest in inventory of the debtor, describing such inventory by item or type.

Note that it is not necessary that the purchase-money secured party obtain the consent of the other secured party who has filed.

The reason for the different requirements for priority with respect to a purchase-money security interest in inventory from the simpler rule covering other collateral was explained in Comment 3 to 1972 § 9-312 as follows:

"Under [1972 § 9-312(3)] the same rule of priority, but without the ten-day grace period for filing, applies to a purchase-money security interest in inventory, with the additional requirement that the purchase-money secured party give notification, as stated in subsection (3), to any other secured party who filed earlier for the same item or type of inventory. The reason for the additional requirement of notification is that typically the arrangement between an inventory secured party and his debtor will require the secured party to make periodic advances against incoming inventory or periodic releases of old inventory as new inventory is received. A fraudulent debtor may apply to the secured party for advances even though he has already given a security interest in the inventory to another secured party. The notification requirement protects the inventory financer in such a situation: if he has received notification, he will presumably not make an advance; if he has not received notification (or if the other interest does not qualify as a purchase-money interest), any advance he may make will have priority. Since an arrangement for periodic advances against incoming property is unusual outside the inventory field, no notification requirement is included in [1972 § 9-312(4)]."

For a similar discussion in the 1999 Code Comments, see Comment 4 to 1999 § 9-324.

Example.   Bank made a loan to Debtor, appliance dealer, secured by all inventory now owned or hereafter acquired. Bank filed a financing statement.   One month later, Finance Company advanced money to Debtor to permit acquisition for resale of inventory manufactured by X. A financing statement covering such X inventory was filed. An officer of Finance Company then telephoned the loan officer of Bank and informed the latter that Finance Company intended to "floor plan" certain X merchandise for Debtor on a "secured money interest." This all took place before any X inventory was delivered to Debtor.   Written or electronic notice would be necessary under the 1999 Code, but the contents of the notice described above should be sufficient.

It should be noted that the 1999 Code has some special provisions regarding purchase-money security interest priority in livestock [1999 § 9-324(d), (e)] and software [1999 § 9-324(f)].

c. Accounts and Proceeds

(1) Purchase-Money Security Interest in Inventory

A priority problem may arise where one person takes a security interest in present and future accounts of a debtor and a different person takes a purchase-money security interest in inventory of the same debtor. When the inventory is sold by the debtor, some form of proceeds results from the sale, which may consist of accounts, chattel paper or payment in the form of cash or checks. Which secured party, the account financer or the inventory purchase-money financer, has priority?

1999 § 9-324(b) resolves the issue by giving the inventory purchase-money secured party priority (if they take the proper steps prescribed in that provision) in chattel paper or instruments constituting proceeds of the inventory; in proceeds of the chattel paper; and in identifiable cash proceeds of the inventory.

Note that, except where the purchase-money inventory financer has priority with respect to proceeds under the 1999 Code, priority as to proceeds is governed by the "first to file or perfect" rule. See § 4a(1) of this chapter.

(2) Purchase-Money Security Interest in Other Collateral

A purchase-money security interest in collateral other than inventory has priority over a conflicting security interest in the same collateral if the purchase-money security interest is perfected at the time the debtor receives possession of the collateral or within 20 days thereafter under the 1999 Code. 1999 § 9-324(a).

When under these rules the purchase-money secured party has priority over another secured party, there is a question whether this priority extends to the proceeds of the original noninventory collateral. The 1999 Code gives the purchase-money secured party priority as to proceeds (whether they are cash or non-cash proceeds), on the basis that there is ordinarily no expectation that such noninventory collateral will be sold.

(3) The "First-to-File-or-Perfect" Rule

In cases where a purchase-money secured party in inventory or other collateral does not obtain priority with respect to proceeds under the rules of 1999 § 9-324(a) or (b), priority as to proceeds is governed by the "first-to-file-or-perfect" rule, described in § 4a(1) of this chapter. This is made clear in 1999 § 9-322(b) which states that for the purposes of the "first-to-file-or-perfect" rule of 1999 § 9-322(a), a date of filing or perfection as to collateral is also a date of filing or perfection as to proceeds. The 1999 Code does add some special rules in this regard applicable to certain types of collateral. See 1999 § 9-322(c) - (e).

d. Where There Is A Consignment

A person who consigns merchandise to another person for resale by the latter runs the risk of losing the consigned goods to the creditors of the consignee. Generally, the safest course for the consignor to take is to file under Article 9, because the 1999 Article 9 includes many consignments within its scope [see 1999 § 9-109(a)(4)]. For discussion of consignments in the light of Article 9, see Chapter 2, § 5e. For discussion of filing where there is a consignment, see Chapter 5, § 11.

In some instances, a consignment may be a secured transaction in the form of inventory financing and thus subject to Article 9 generally. Filing by such a consignor gives them a perfected security interest. Since the consignor has a purchase-money security interest in the consigned goods as inventory in the hands of the consignee, they may protect against claims of other secured parties with perfected security interests in the consignee's inventory by taking the steps outlined in 1999 § 9-324(b), that is, by filing before the consignee receives the consigned goods and by giving appropriate notice to other inventory secured parties who have filed. See § 4b(2) of this chapter.

In some other instances, a "true consignment" is not intended as a secured transaction, although the consignor may still file under Article 9 in order to protect their interest against creditors of the consignee. What are the rights of such a consignor who files, as against another person who has a perfected security interest in the inventory of the consignee, which inventory includes the consigned goods?

Third persons, such as other secured parties or creditors of the consignee are in much the same position, whether a consignment is intended as a secured transaction or not. Accordingly, 1999 §§ 9-103(d) and 9-324(b) set forth additional steps to be taken by a consignor in a true consignment transaction in order to obtain priority over a secured party who has filed with respect to inventory, including the consigned goods. The steps to be taken are the same as those required of a secured party with a purchase-money security interest in inventory under 1999 § 9-324(b). In other words, the consignor must file before the consignee receives possession of the goods, and must give written notification to any other secured party who has filed. The notification must state that the consignor expects to deliver goods on consignment to the consignee, and describe the goods by item or type. The notification must be given within five years before the consignee receives the goods.

e. Other Priority Rules

1999 § 9-322(f) makes cross references to other priority rules, indicating that Part 3 of 1999 Article 9 otherwise sets forth the priority rules that govern security interests.

(1) Reference is made to § 9-322(g) which gives preemptive effect to separate statutory law from UCC Article 9 that governs priority of agricultural liens.

(2) Reference is made to § 4-210, which states that the security interest obtained by a bank in an item and accompanying documents handled by the bank for collection has priority over conflicting perfected security interests.

(3) Reference is made to § 5-118 which is given effect with respect to the security interest of an

issuer of a letter of credit or a nominated person. § 5-118 is added by the 1999 Code and gives a security interest to an issuer of a letter of credit in a document presented under the letter of credit to the extent that the issuer honors or gives value for the presentation.

(4) Reference is made to security interests arising under UCC Article 2 or 2A in 1999 § 9-110. See discussion of 1999 § 9-110 in the next section of this chapter.

§ 5.   Unpaid Seller of Goods

In certain instances, an unpaid seller of goods may have a claim to the goods against one who has a perfected security interest extending to such goods, which interest is given by the buyer. The controversy may arise where a buyer of goods has granted a security interest to a lender in all of the buyer's inventory and all after-acquired inventory and where either of the following two situations occurs: (1) a seller sells goods that become part of the buyer's inventory for cash and is paid by the buyer's check which is dishonored for insufficient funds, or (2) a seller sells the goods that become part of the buyer's inventory on credit but discovers that the buyer is insolvent.

The first situation is a cash sale. The buyer's right as against the seller to retain or dispose of the goods is conditional upon the buyer's making the payment due, under § 2-507(2). Payment by check is conditional and is defeated as between the parties by dishonor of the check on due presentment, under § 2-511(3).

The second situation is a sale on credit. Under § 2-702(2) and (3), the seller has a right to reclaim the goods upon discovering the insolvency of the buyer on credit, but the seller must normally act within 10 days of receipt by the buyer of the goods.

The 1972 Code did not have a clear answer as to whether the unpaid seller's interest has priority over a security interest granted by the buyer in after-acquired property. In either of the above situations, it would seem that the cash or credit seller should be able to get the goods back against the claim of a secured party of the buyer who has a perfected security interest in the goods as after-acquired property. In particular, it would seem that the seller should prevail if a demand for them is made within 10 days of receipt by the buyer. See § 2-702(2) and Comment 3 to § 2-507, indicating that the 10-day rule also applies in the case of a cash sale, as well as a credit sale. However, case law generally favored the buyer's secured party in such a situation. For a leading case, see In re Samuels & Co., Inc. 526 F.2d 1238 (5th Cir. 1976), applying Texas law.

The 1999 Code also does not provide a clear answer to this priority problem. Section 9-110 makes reference to some UCC Article 2 and 2A provisions, providing that security interests created by those provisions are subject to 1999 Article 9. The § 9-110 Code Comments appear to reject the above-referenced case law that gives Article 9 secured parties priority over the unpaid seller's claim to the goods. See Comment 5 to 1999 § 9-110.

For discussion of the right of the unpaid seller for cash or on credit as against the buyer's trustee in bankruptcy, see Chapter 8, § 10.

§ 6.   Priority Between Secured Party and Lien Creditor

a. General Rule

The Code does not expressly deal with priority between a secured party with a perfected security interest and a creditor who has subsequently obtained a lien on the collateral by attachment, garnishment, levy or the like. However, it is clearly implied that the secured party with a prior perfected interest should prevail over a subsequent lien creditor, since 1999 § 9-317(a)(2) makes an unperfected security interest subordinate to the rights of a person who becomes a lien creditor before the security interest is perfected. See discussion in § 2a of this chapter.

In other words, if the secured party files or otherwise perfects before the creditor obtains a lien, the secured party has priority. On the other hand, if the creditor obtains a lien before the secured party files or otherwise perfects, the creditor has priority.

CAVEAT. Some state statutes outside the Uniform Commercial Code set forth liens of various kinds which take priority over even an earlier, perfected security interest. Statutes of that nature are varied in scope from state to state.

Note: Federal tax liens can also have priority in certain instances over prior perfected security interests. In addition, some perfected security interests can be set aside in a federal bankruptcy proceeding. For discussion of federal tax liens, see § 6c of this chapter. For discussion of the effect of bankruptcy on a security interest, see Chapter 8 generally.

b. Future Advances by Secured Party

The 1999 Code gives priority to a subsequent lien creditor against a prior perfected security interest to the extent of certain future advances made by the secured party. Specifically, 1999 Article 9 provides that a person who becomes a lien creditor while a security interest is perfected takes subject to the security interest only to the extent that it secures advances made before they became a lien creditor or within 45 days thereafter or made without knowledge of the lien or pursuant to a commitment entered into without knowledge of the lien. 1999 § 9-323(b).

Comment 4 to 1999 § 9-323 points out that the purpose of 1999 § 9-323(b) is to give a perfected security interest priority with respect to future advances for 45 days after a lien is obtained on the collateral, without regard to knowledge of the lien on the part of the secured party. Even after 45 days, the secured party has priority if they make the advance without knowledge of the lien. Presumably, actual knowledge is necessary; knowledge should not be imputed by reason of the filing of a judgment lien or the like.

This provision of the 1999 Code dovetails with the 45-day provision of the Federal Tax Lien Act, which is discussed immediately below.

c. Federal Tax Lien

If any person liable to pay any tax to the United States neglects or refuses to pay the same after demand, the amount (including interest and other additions) shall be a lien in favor of the United States upon all property belonging to such person. The lien arises at the time the assessment is made, demand for payment of the tax occurs, and the taxpayer fails to pay the taxes. 26 U.S.C.A. § 6321. The priority of the lien as against third-party claims generally, relates back to the time of assessment of the tax. 26 U.S.C.A. § 6322. However, the lien is not valid as against the holder of a security interest until appropriate notice of the lien is filed. See 26 U.S.C.A. 6323(a).

Filing of a federal tax lien may be made in any place designated by the law of the state where the property subject to the lien is situated, or with the clerk of the local United States District Court if no such state law exists. See 26 U.S.C.A. § 6323(f). Most states have statutes permitting the filing of a federal tax lien in some state, county or other local office.

The federal tax lien is declared in 26 U.S.C.A. § 6323(a) to be inferior to the interest of any purchaser, holder of a security interest, mechanic's lienor or judgment lien creditor until notice of the tax lien has been filed. In other words, if an Article 9 security interest is perfected on a taxpayer's property prior to the time the notice of tax lien is filed, the security interest is given priority over the tax lien.

26 U.S.C.A. § 6323(c) limits priority of the security interest with regard to collateral acquired after the notice of tax lien is filed that becomes subject to a secured party's UCC Article 9 security interest because of an after-acquired property clause in the security agreement. As to such after-acquired collateral, 26 U.S.C.A. § 6323(c) provides for priority of the security interest only if the secured party perfected its security interest prior to the filing of the federal tax lien and made any loans to the taxpayer without knowledge of the tax lien; the collateral must be "commercial financing security," i.e., accounts, chattel paper or instruments; and the collateral must have been acquired within 45 days of the filing of the notice of the federal tax lien.

26 U.S.C.A. § 6323(d) further limits priority of the security interest as to future advances made by the secured party after notice of the tax lien has been filed. In order to have priority as to such advances, the secured party must have perfected its security interest prior to the filing of the notice of the tax lien and the advance must have been made within 45

days after the filing of the notice of the tax lien or before the secured party obtained knowledge of the federal tax lien filing, whichever first occurs.

d. Artisan's or Repairman's Lien

When a person in the ordinary course of their business furnishes services or materials with respect to goods subject to a security interest, a lien upon goods in the possession of such person given by statute or rule of law for such materials or services takes priority over a perfected security interest unless the lien is statutory and the statute expressly provides otherwise. 1999 § 9-333.

The above Code provision recognizes that most states have so-called "artisan's lien" statutes which accord to a repairman a lien on goods in their possession for the cost of repairs made or materials used in making repairs. The repairman has a right to payment before being required to surrender the goods to the owner.

1999 § 9-333 gives the repairman's lien priority over even a perfected security interest, in the absence of a statute expressly making the repairman's lien subordinate. The reason for the Code provision is that such liens deserve priority, since the repairman's work has enhanced or preserved the value of the collateral.

There is no requirement of consent on the part of the secured party that the repairs be made. However, the superiority of the lien over the security interest depends on possession of the goods by the repairman; if they surrender possession before being paid, their lien is subordinate to the perfected security interest.

§ 7.   Priority of Security Interest in Fixtures

Significant issues related to priority of claims in fixtures are dealt with in the 1999 § 9-334. These issues involve the relative priority between a person with a security interest in fixtures and one or more competing real estate interests. Such real estate interests might include the interest of an owner of the real estate (other than the debtor) where the fixtures are installed, the interest of a mortgagee of the real estate, the interest of one who has a judgment lien on the real estate or the interest of a subsequent purchaser of the real estate. For a definition of "fixtures," see Chapter 1, § 7a(5).

The 1999 Code makes it clear in its "filing provisions" (1999 §§ 9-501 et seq.) that a fixture filing must be made not only at the office where a mortgage on the real estate would be filed or recorded, but also that the filing must be made in the real estate records of that office in such a way as to permit one searching the real estate title to locate the filing.

The provisions of the 1999 Code relating to priority are summarized as follows:

(1) In general, priority over real estate interests is largely governed by a fixture filing, or in some instances by perfection in some other manner.

(2) A purchase-money security interest in fixtures has priority over the conflicting interest of an encumbrancer or owner arising before the goods become fixtures, if the security interest is perfected by a fixture filing before the goods become fixtures or within 20 days thereafter. 1999 § 9-334(d). The debtor must either have an interest of record in the real estate or be in possession.

In other words, the holder of a purchase-money security interest (which most security interests in fixtures would be) has a 20-day grace period after installation of the fixture within which to make an effective fixture filing. The requirement that the debtor have an interest of record in the real estate or be in possession makes it clear that a fixture secured party may not defeat real estate interests by taking a security interest against a contractor who has no interest of record or is not in possession. On the other hand, a fixture filing may be made where the debtor is a lessee in possession of the real estate if the name of a record owner is given in the filing. 1999 § 9-502(b)(4).

(3) A security interest in fixtures has priority if it is perfected by a fixture filing before the interest of the encumbrancer or owner is of record, the security interest has priority over any conflicting interest of a predecessor in title of the encumbrancer or owner, and the debtor has an interest of record or is in possession of the real estate. This rule basically gives priority according to the usual priority rule of real estate conveyancing, that is, the first to file or record prevails. The apparent limitation that the secured party must have priority over any interest of a predecessor in title of the conflicting interest is merely an expression of the usual rule that a person must be entitled to transfer what they have. 1999 § 9-334(e)(1).

Example 1. A purchase-money security interest is not filed as a fixture filing within 20 days after the fixture is installed. It is thus subordinate to the interest of a prior recorded mortgage. It is also subordinate to the interest of an assignee of the mortgage even though the assignment is recorded after the fixture filing is made.

Example 2. A purchase-money security interest is filed as a fixture filing within 20 days after the fixture is installed. It is thus superior to the interest of a prior recorded mortgage. It is also superior to the interest of an assignee of the mortgage or to the interest of any subsequent mortgagee or purchaser of the real estate, which interest is recorded after the fixture filing is made.

(4) A security interest has priority if the fixtures are readily removable factory or office machines or readily removable replacements of domestic appliances which are consumer goods, and before the goods become fixtures, the security interest is perfected by any method permitted under Article 9. 1999 § 9-334(e)(2)(A), (C). In other words, a secured party need not file a fixture filing with respect to readily removable factory or office machines to have priority, but may file with respect to ordinary equipment as a chattel filing. Under 1999 § 9-334 (e)(2)(B) the same rule applies to equipment that is not primarily used or leased for use in the operation of the real property. Where the replacements of domestic appliances are consumer goods, a secured party need not file at all, since perfection takes place automatically upon attachment of the security interest under 1999 § 9-309(1).

(5) A security interest in fixtures has priority if the conflicting interest is a lien on the real estate obtained by legal or equitable proceedings after the security interest was perfected by any method permitted under Article 9, i.e., filing a financing statement or filing a fixture filing. 1999 § 9-334(e)(3). This recognizes that a judgment lien creditor is not a "reliance creditor" who would have searched records. Moreover, the provision is intended to make certain that a security interest in a fixture which is perfected in any manner should be considered as perfected in the event of subsequent bankruptcy of the debtor. See Comment 9 to 1999 § 9-334. This should protect a perfected security interest from a claim under the "strong-arm" clause of the Bankruptcy Code, no matter how the interest was perfected. For discussion of the "strong-arm" clause, see Chapter 8, § 4.

Example 3. Debtor purchases a new heating/air-conditioning unit for installation on their business premises. Although the unit is a fixture, Secured Party who has a purchase-money security interest in the unit files in the office or offices where a filing should be made on ordinary chattels as equipment. Creditor subsequently obtains a judgment lien on the real estate where the unit is installed. Although Secured Party did not make a fixture filing, they have a perfected security interest good against

Creditor. Note that if the unit had been installed as a replacement of a similar unit in a home, the security interest could be perfected without filing and would be good against any encumbrancer or owner of the home.

(6) A security interest in fixtures, whether or not perfected, has priority over the conflicting interest of an encumbrancer or owner who has consented in writing to the security interest or has disclaimed an interest in the goods as fixtures. The security interest also has priority if the debtor has a right to remove the goods as against the encumbrancer or owner. 1999 § 9-334(f). This latter provision should apply in a case where the fixture is installed on land leased by the debtor and where the lease permits the debtor to remove the fixture.

(7) A purchase-money security interest in fixtures is subordinate to a construction mortgage which is recorded before the goods become fixtures if the goods become fixtures before completion of the construction. A subsequent mortgage given to refinance the construction mortgage has the same priority. 1999 § 9-334(h). The reason for giving priority to the construction mortgagee is to prevent the double-financing of fixtures where funds to purchase the goods are obtained from the mortgagee and the fixtures are then purchased on credit from a

supplier.   The latter who sells on credit for installation in a house or building under construction should protect their interest by checking the real estate records before allowing the credit sale. Note that this rule does not apply where additions are made to a building after completion of the improvement and are financed under an "open-end" clause of a construction mortgage or refinancing mortgage. See Comment 11 to 1999 § 9-334.

(8) In any case not specified above, a security interest in fixtures is subordinate to the conflicting interest of an encumbrancer or owner of the related real estate who is not the debtor. 1999 § 9-334(c).

(9) Article 9 does not prevent creation of an encumbrance upon fixtures pursuant to real estate law.   1999 § 9-334(b).   However, note that a recorded real estate mortgage is ineffective to cover nonfixture personal property on the mortgaged premises, as against the interest of a secured party. A mortgagee desiring to cover such nonfixture property should take action to perfect their interest under Article 9, as by filing in the chattel records.

The 1999 Code adds special provisions dealing with manufactured homes. Generally, a security interest in a manufactured home has priority over an encumbrancer or owner if the security interest is created pursuant to statutory law separate from the

Code. See 1999 §§ 9-334(e)(4); 9-311(a)(2); 9-102(a)(53), (54).

The 1999 Code also indicates that a perfected security interest in crops growing on real property has priority over a conflicting interest of an encumbrancer or owner of the real property if the debtor has an interest of record or is in possession of the real property. 1999 § 9-334(i).

§ 8. Priority of Security Interest in Accessions

In certain instances, a security interest may be taken in goods which are installed or affixed to other goods, which are called "accessions," such as a new motor installed in an automobile. Another person may have a competing claim to the whole of the goods in which the accession is installed, such as a person with a security interest in the automobile in which the new motor is installed.

1999 § 9-335 sets forth rules of priority between a secured party with an interest in an accession and a competing claim to the whole goods. The 1999 Code provides a definition of "accession." Accordingly, an accession means goods that are physically united with other goods in such a manner that the identity of the original goods is not lost. 1999 § 9-102(a)(1). A good is an accession regardless of the cost or difficulty of removing the accession from the other goods and regardless of whether the original goods have come to form an integral part of the other goods; however, if the identity of the goods is lost, the good is not an accession and 1999 § 9-335 is inapplicable. See Comment 2 to § 9-335. If a security interest is perfected in goods when the goods become an accession, the security interest remains perfected thereafter. 1999 § 9-335(a), (b).

Subject to only one exception, the 1999 Code indicates that the priority rules governing priority of a security interest found in other provisions of Part 3 of 1999 Article 9 will apply. Thus, for example, when appropriate, the first-to-file-or-perfect rule of 1999 § 9-322(a)(1) or the purchase-money security rule of 1999 § 9-324(a) will apply. The one exception involves certificate-of-title collateral. A security interest in an accession is subordinate to a security interest in the whole which is perfected by compliance with certificate-of-title statutes. 1999 §§ 9-335(d), 9-311(b).

§ 9.   Priority When Goods are Commingled or Processed

A debtor might grant a security interest in goods

to one creditor and thereafter commingle those goods with others in which the debtor had granted a security interest to another creditor. Under 1999 § 9-336(a)-(d), a security interest does not exist in commingled goods but does attach to a product or mass when goods are physically united with other goods in a manner that their identity is lost in the product or mass; if the security interest was perfected in goods before commingling, the security interest remains perfected in the product or mass.

Where more than one security interest attaches to the product or mass, they rank equally according to the ratio that the cost of the goods to which each interest originally attached bears to the cost of the total product or mass. 1999 § 9-336(f)(2).

The above rules apply not only to processing where raw materials lose their identity when processed into finished goods, but also where components are assembled into a machine. See Comment 2 to 1999 § 9-336, which gives as an example ball bearings in a machine.

§ 10. Priority When Goods are Returned or Repossessed

A priority problem may sometimes arise where there are conflicting security interests with respect to returned or repossessed goods. In some instances, a seller of goods may finance their inventory with one secured party. When they sell an item of inventory other than for cash, an account may arise or chattel paper may be given by the debtor to the seller. The seller may then assign the account or chattel paper to a second secured party. If the goods are later returned to the seller by the buyer voluntarily for any reason or are repossessed by the seller (which may be done under 1999 §§ 9-205 if they handle their own collections), a conflict may arise between the inventory secured party and the secured party taking the assignment of the account or chattel paper.

The 1999 Code deals with such conflicting security interests in 1999 § 9-330. See Comments 9-11 to 1999 § 9-330. The rules may be summarized as follows:

(1) The inventory secured party with a security interest in the goods before sale automatically has a security interest in the returned goods if the original debt is unpaid. If the security interest had been perfected at the time of sale by a still-effective filing, it remains perfected automatically upon return of the goods; otherwise, the secured party must take possession of the returned goods or must file.

(2) An unpaid transferee of chattel paper taken when the goods were sold has priority with respect

to the returned goods over the inventory secured party if the chattel paper transferee had priority over the inventory secured party with respect to the chattel paper itself.

(3) An unpaid transferee of an account arising after the sale of the goods has a security interest in the returned goods subordinate to the interest of the inventory secured party, if the latter's security interest is perfected.

(4) An unpaid transferee of chattel paper or an account must perfect their security interest in the returned goods for protection against creditors of the seller-transferor and purchasers of the returned or repossessed goods. In other words, the unpaid transferee must file or take possession of the returned goods; their security interest does not automatically carry over to the returned goods as does the security interest of the inventory secured party.

Note, however, that if the seller again sells the returned goods to a second buyer who is a buyer in the ordinary course of business, the buyer is fully protected against either the inventory secured party or the secured party having an interest in the chattel paper or account.

§ 11. Investment Property

The 1999 Code provides special priority rules when the collateral is investment property. 1999 § 9-328. For a general discussion of investment property and perfection of security interests therein, see Chapter 4, § 4b and Chapter 1, § 9a(3).

Under 1999 § 9-328, a security interest in investment property perfected by control (1999 § 9-106) has priority over a security interest held by another who does not have control of the investment property. When both conflicting security interests have control, the priority is determined on the basis of which party first obtained control; that party is given priority.

§ 12. Deposit Accounts Under the 1999 Code

The 1999 Code governs secured transactions when the collateral is a non-consumer deposit account. See 1999 §§ 9-109(a), (d)(13); 9-102(a) (29) and discussion at Chapter 1, § 7. As a result, priority rules are included to deal with priority disputes involving deposit accounts.

A security interest perfected by control of a deposit account has priority over a conflicting security interest of another secured party who does not have control. 1999 § 9-327(1). Perfection by control is considered in Chapter 4, § 12a. If both security interests are perfected by control, they rank according to priority in time of obtaining control. 1999 § 9-327(2). On the other hand, a security interest held by the bank at which the account is maintained has priority over another secured party's security interest unless that secured party perfected it's security interest by control, in which case that security interest is given priority. 1999 § 9-327(3), (4). If funds are transferred from a deposit account, usually the transferee will take free of the security interest in the account. 1999 § 9-332(b).

A separate priority issue involving deposit accounts arises when a secured party has a security interest in a debtor's account or can trace proceeds from other collateral into the account. If the depositary bank has made a loan to the debtor-account holder and that loan is in default, the bank has a common-law right to set off the loan against the account. The issue arises as to who has priority in the account—the bank asserting its setoff right or the UCC Article 9 secured party. The 1999 Code provides that the bank has priority unless the secured party has perfected its security interest by control, in which case the secured party is given priority. 1999 § 9-340. See also related 1999 §§ 9-341, 9-342.

§ 13. Letter-of-Credit Rights Under the 1999 Code

The 1999 Code governs secured transactions when the collateral is a letter-of-credit right. See 1999 §§ 9-109(a), 9-102(a)(51), and discussion at Chapter 1, § 7 and Chapter 4, § 12a. As a result, priority rules are included to deal with priority disputes over letter-of-credit rights. It should be noted that the 1999 Code is inapplicable to the extent that the rights of a transferee beneficiary or nominated person under a letter of credit are independent and superior under § 5-114.

A security interest perfected by control of a letter-of-credit right has priority over a conflicting interest of another secured party who does not have control. 1999 § 9-329(1). Perfection by control is considered in Chapter 4, § 12a. If both security interests are perfected by control, they rank according to priority in time of obtaining control. 1999 § 9-329(2).

§ 14. Agricultural Liens Under the 1999 Code

The 1999 Code includes agricultural liens within its scope. 1999 §§ 9-109(a)(2), 9-102(a)(5). For discussion of agricultural liens as included within the scope of the 1999 Code, see Chapter 1, § 3 and Chapter 4, § 12b.

The inclusion of agricultural liens within 1999 Article 9 necessitated inclusion of priority rules applicable to such liens. For the most part, the priority rules applicable to unperfected and perfected security interests also apply to agricultural liens. For example, such rules include the first-to-file-or-perfect rule of 1999 § 9-322(a). For discussion of this rule, see § 4a(1) of this chapter. However, 1999 § 9-322(g) provides that a perfected agricultural lien on collateral has priority over a security interest in or agricultural lien on the same collateral if the statute creating the agricultural lien so provides. In other words, the statute creating the agricultural lien can preempt application of the usual Code priority rules. See also Comment 12 to 1999 § 9-322.

§ 15. "Double-Debtor Problem" Under the 1999 Code

Sometimes a debtor acquires property that is subject to a security interest created by another debtor.

Example. Adams owns an item of equipment subject to a security interest that Adam granted to Old Bank. Adams sells the equipment to Baker, the latter taking the equipment subject to Old Bank's security interest. Baker then grants a security interest to New Bank. Who has priority to the equipment—Old Bank or New Bank?

The 1999 Code usually gives priority to Old Bank. 1999 § 9-325(a) gives Old Bank priority as long as Old Bank's security interest was perfected when Baker acquired the equipment and remained perfected subsequently. There are some exceptions to this priority rule but those exceptions apply only in unusual situations. See 1999 § 9-325(b) and Comment 6 to 1999 § 9-325.

§ 16. Priority of Security Interests Created by a "New Debtor" Under the 1999 Code

The 1999 Code addresses the priority issues that arise when a new debtor becomes bound by a security agreement of an original debtor but where each debtor has a secured creditor.

Example. Old Bank has acquired a security interest in Adams' existing and after-acquired inventory. Old Bank perfected by filing a financing statement. New Bank has acquired a perfected security interest in Baker's existing and after-acquired inventory. New Bank perfected by filing a financing statement. Baker later becomes bound as debtor by Adams' security agreement because Baker has acquired Adams' business and has assumed

Adams' debtor to Old Bank. Subsequently, Baker acquires a new item of inventory. Who has priority in the new item of inventory—Old Bank or New Bank?

Under the 1999 Code at § 9-508, Old Bank's financing statement is effective to perfect a security interest in the new item of inventory in which Baker has rights. However, 1999 § 9-326(a) gives priority to New Bank regardless of whether New Bank filed its financing statement before Old Bank filed its financing statement. See Comment 1 to 1999 § 9-326, Example 2.

CHAPTER 8

BANKRUPTCY OR INSOLVENCY OF DEBTOR

§ 1. General Effect of Insolvency

In some instances, the debtor in a secured transaction may become insolvent. Under pre-revision § 1-201(23), a person is "insolvent" who "either has ceased to pay his debts in the ordinary course of business or cannot pay his debts as they become due or is insolvent within the meaning of the federal bankruptcy law." Similarly, revised § 1-201(b)(23) defines "insolvent" to mean "having generally ceased to pay debts in the ordinary course of business other than as a result of a bona fide dispute ... being unable to pay debts as they become due ... or being insolvent within the meaning of federal bankruptcy law." In many instances, when a debtor becomes insolvent, some form of "insolvency proceedings" may ensue. That term is defined in pre-revision § 1-201(22) and revised § 1-201(b)(22) as including "an assignment for the benefit of creditors or other proceeding intended to liquidate or rehabilitate the estate of the person involved."

Insolvency proceedings may be instituted by or against an insolvent debtor under either state law or under the federal Bankruptcy Code. Normally, federal bankruptcy procedures will be utilized. However, where state law is utilized, there may be an informal arrangement between the debtor and creditors, including a composition with creditors or an extension of time of payment, or both. The debtor may also make an assignment for the benefit of creditors or the court may appoint a receiver to manage the debtor's assets on behalf of their creditors. Note that 1999 § 9-102(a)(52) declares that an assignee for the benefit of creditors is a lien creditor from the time of assignment and a receiver in equity is a lien creditor from the time of appointment. Such a representative of creditors has lien creditor status even though the creditors represented are general creditors and not lien creditors.

It follows that an assignee for the benefit of creditors or a receiver has priority as a lien creditor over an unperfected security interest under 1999 § 9-317(a)(2). See Chapter 7, § 2a.

Conversely, a security interest which has been perfected at the time an assignment for the benefit of creditors is made or at the time a receiver is appointed has priority over the subsequent lien of the assignee or receiver. Note, however, that there is a possibility of attacking a perfected security interest as a fraudulent transfer under state law where the value of the collateral is substantially disproportionate to the debt secured or where there are other facts indicating that the interest is taken in fraud of other creditors of the debtor. See Uniform Fraudulent Transfer Act § 4.

§ 2.   A Brief Summary of Federal Bankruptcy Law

a. The Statute

Some knowledge of federal bankruptcy law is necessary when considering the impact of bankruptcy on a secured transaction. The summary here is necessarily brief; other sources should be consulted for general discussion of bankruptcy law. Among such sources, see Epstein, BANKRUPTCY AND RELATED LAW IN A NUTSHELL, 7th ed.

The law of bankruptcy is federal law under U.S. Constitution Art. 1, § 8, cl. 4. Bankruptcy statutes have often referred to state law or permitted the use of state law for particular purposes, such as UCC Article 9. For many years, bankruptcy and certain proceedings directed toward rehabilitation of a debtor in financial straits were governed by the

Bankruptcy Act of 1898, referred to in this Nutshell as the "1898 Act." In 1978, Congress enacted a new statute known as the "Bankruptcy Reform Act of 1978." The new act is referred to in this Nutshell as the "Bankruptcy Code." References to the "Code" are to the Uniform Commercial Code. The Bankruptcy Code completely replaced the 1898 Act and applies to bankruptcy proceedings commenced on or after October 1, 1979. The substantive provisions of the Bankruptcy Code are in Title I, codified in revised Title 11 U.S.C.A. Congress has amended the Bankruptcy Code in 1984, 1986, 1988, 1990, 1992, 1994 and 2005. References in this Nutshell to sections of the Bankruptcy Code as amended are to those sections as codified in 11 U.S.C.A. For example, a reference to Bankruptcy Code § 547 is to 11 U.S.C.A. § 547.

One of the reasons a creditor obtains a security interest in the debtor's property is to better the creditor's prospects of collection if the debtor ends up in bankruptcy. However, it may be said that the lot of the secured party in an Article 9 transaction is not always a particularly happy one, where the debtor files bankruptcy or an involuntary bankruptcy proceeding is filed by creditors against a debtor under the Bankruptcy Code. Bankruptcy has far-reaching effects on an Article 9 security interest. At the worst, the security interest may be set aside or rendered ineffective, with the secured party relegated to the position of an unsecured general creditor of the insolvent debtor. Even at best, as where the security interest is "impregnably" perfected, the secured party is usually subject to the jurisdiction of the bankruptcy court and sometimes to the whims of the debtor's trustee in bankruptcy in dealing with the collateral. In short, the remedies of the secured party under 1999 § 9-601 et seq. are considerably curtailed as against a bankrupt debtor. Various problems of bankruptcy as affecting secured transactions are discussed in detail in the balance of this chapter of the Nutshell.

b. *The General Nature of Bankruptcy*

The traditional aim of bankruptcy has been to enable an impecunious debtor to "get a new start in life" at least in a financial sense. The Bankruptcy Code contemplates that a bankrupt individual debtor may obtain, in most instances, a discharge of most (though not necessarily all) debts owed. A "discharge" means that the debtor need not pay their debts except to the extent required in the bankruptcy proceeding; that is, the debtor's personal liability terminates as to the debts existing at the commencement of a bankruptcy. See Bankruptcy Code § 727. This is frequently accomplished through the appointment of a trustee who gathers together and converts into cash the debtor's non-exempt assets for ratable distribution to creditors in accordance with a statutory scheme of priorities. It follows that many bankruptcy cases are *liquidation* proceedings (or "straight bankruptcy" cases under the former law) governed by Bankruptcy Code Chapter 7, § 701 et seq.

In some instances, *rehabilitation* of the debtor is the objective, rather than liquidation and distribution to creditors of the debtor's nonexempt assets. The creditors look more to future earnings of the debtor to satisfy claims in whole or in part. Bankruptcy Code Chapter 11, § 1101 et seq., deals with rehabilitation or reorganization of a business debtor, who may be an individual or an entity such as a corporation or partnership.

Rehabilitation is also the objective in a proceeding under Bankruptcy Code Chapter 13, § 1301 et seq., which provides for adjustment of the debts of an individual with "regular income" and obligations of fixed unsecured debts of less than $301,675 and of fixed secured debts of less than $922.975. These amounts will be changed from time to time.

A third rehabilitation procedure is provided for at Bankruptcy Code Chapter 12, § 1201 et seq. It provides for adjustment of debts of a family farmer with regular income and will not be considered in this Nutshell. Chapter 12 is in large part patterned after Bankruptcy Code Chapter 13.

General provisions of the Bankruptcy Code, Chapters 1, 3 and 5, §§ 101 et seq., 301 et seq. and 501 et seq., apply to liquidation cases under Chapter 7 and rehabilitation cases under Chapters 11 or 13 unless otherwise specified. There is also a Bankruptcy Code Chapter 9, § 901 et seq. dealing with adjustment of debts of a municipality, which should rarely if ever affect secured transactions under Uniform Commercial Code Article 9. Note that under 1999 § 9-109(c)(2) and (3), UCC Article 9 applies to security interests created by a State, foreign country, or a governmental unit of either, except to the extent that another statute governs the issue in question.

Bankruptcy cases are heard in *bankruptcy courts* which exist in each federal judicial district as a unit of a federal district court. The cases and proceedings that arise within the cases are referred by the district court to the bankruptcy court. 28 USCA §§ 151, 157, 1334. A district court has broad jurisdiction over all of the property, wherever located, of the debtor, as of the time of commencement of the case. The court has broad powers covering virtually all aspects of bankruptcy. The judge of a bankruptcy court is called a *bankruptcy judge* (at one time they were called bankruptcy referees). The powers of a bankruptcy judge are somewhat limited under the Bankruptcy Code due to the fact bankruptcy judges are not given the protections required by Article III of the United States Constitution of tenure for life and the like.

Most Bankruptcy Code cases start with filing by the debtor of a *voluntary petition* under Chapter 7 or, in some instances, Chapter 11, 12 or 13. See Bankruptcy Code § 301. In certain instances, creditors of a debtor may file an *involuntary petition* against a debtor under Chapter 7 or Chapter 11, but not under Chapter 12 or 13. See Bankruptcy Code § 303. The petition is filed in the bankruptcy court and the case is then commenced. *The time of filing of the petition is the time of the bankruptcy.*

The next event after the filing of a petition is a meeting of creditors under Bankruptcy Code § 341. This meeting usually results in election by the creditors of a *trustee*, if the proceeding is a liquidation case. See Bankruptcy Code § 702.

The trustee is essentially a creature of federal law acting as a representative of general creditors, and having various statutory duties and powers. In a liquidation proceeding, the general duties of the trustee are to "collect and reduce to money the property of the estate for which such trustee serves, and close such estate as expeditiously as is compatible with the best interests of parties in interest." Bankruptcy Code § 704(1). In this connection, "property of the estate" is described in seven numbered subparagraphs of Bankruptcy Code § 541 (a). This includes, under Bankruptcy Code § 541(a)(1), "all legal or equitable interests of the debtor in property as of the commencement of the case." Thus, it is clear that property of the estate includes the debtor's property subject to a security interest, even if the interest is perfected. Whether the debtor or secured party has "title" to the collateral is irrelevant. In this connection, see 1999 § 9-202.

In a Chapter 11 proceeding, the debtor ordinarily remains in possession of the property of the estate and assumes most of the powers of the trustee. See Bankruptcy Code § 1107. Although no trustee is appointed in most instances, one may be appointed; and where no trustee is appointed, an examiner with somewhat limited powers may be appointed. See Bankruptcy Code § 1104.

In a Chapter 13 case, the court appoints the trustee and there may be a "standing trustee" named by the court to handle Chapter 13 cases in the judicial district. See Bankruptcy Code § 1302.

Although liquidation under Chapter 7 ordinarily results in disposition of collateral subject to a security interest (see § 3d of this chapter of the Nutshell), the debtor in a Chapter 11, 12 or 13 proceeding is often allowed to retain and use the collateral, even where the secured obligation is in default. The reason is that such a rehabilitation proceeding often takes the form of extension of the time of payment and perhaps scaling down the indebtedness. Continued use of the collateral by the debtor is often necessary to permit the carrying out of the rehabilitation plan. Even in a Chapter 7 liquidation, there may be instances where it is advantageous to permit continued use of the collateral on behalf of the debtor's estate for a limited period.

§ 3.   General Effect on Secured Transactions

a. Stay of Enforcement of Security Interest

Bankruptcy Code § 362(a) provides for an "automatic stay." It is effective upon the filing of a bankruptcy petition. This is very broad in scope and bars virtually all collection efforts against the debtor. *Thus, any act which a secured party might take against a debtor or the debtor's property is automatically suspended or barred, upon the filing of a petition under Bankruptcy Code Chapters 7, 11, 12 or 13.* A secured party may not collect the debt, obtain or enforce a judgment, make a setoff, repossess the collateral or perfect a security interest (except as indicated below).

Bankruptcy Code § 362(b) sets forth some exceptions to the automatic stay. This includes the right of a secured party to perfect a security interest if such perfection would, under state law, be retroactive to a date before the filing of the petition. Bankruptcy Code §§ 362(b)(3) and 546(b). This means that a security interest may be perfected by filing within 20 days under the 1999 Code after the debtor receives possession of the collateral even if such perfection by filing takes place after the filing of the petition under the Bankruptcy Code. Thus, the Bankruptcy Code substantially adopts the 20-day rule of 1999 § 9-317(e) applicable to purchase-money security interests.

Example. Debtor gives a purchase-money security interest, receives possession of the collateral on May 1 and files a bankruptcy petition on May 6. Secured party may effectively file a financing statement on or before May 20, even with knowledge of the bankruptcy filing, assuming that the uniform 20-day grace period of 1999 § 9-317(e) is enacted in the applicable state.

Provision is made in Bankruptcy Code § 362(d)-(g) for relief under certain circumstances from the automatic stay. A secured party may request such relief as a "party in interest" and the court shall grant it for cause, including the lack of "adequate protection" of the security interest. See Bankruptcy Code § 362(d)(1). The issue of "adequate protection" is covered in Bankruptcy Code § 361. This permits protection of a secured party's interest by such means as periodic cash payments to the extent of a decrease in value of the collateral, an additional or replacement lien, or other relief (except allowance of compensation as an "administrative expense") as will result in the realization of the "indubitable equivalent" of the interest in the property. The meaning of "indubitable equivalent" is not clear and it is the function of the bankruptcy court to decide what is an "indubitable equivalent" in a particular case.

Relief may also be granted from the automatic stay if "the debtor does not have an equity" in the collateral, as where the secured debt exceeds the value of the collateral, and the property "is not necessary to an effective reorganization." Bankruptcy Code § 362(d)(2). A stay is terminated 30 days after the request is made unless the court takes other action. Provision is made for a preliminary hearing and a final hearing by the court and for a continuation of the stay or early relief from the stay under certain circumstances. Bankruptcy Code § 362(e) and (f).

The party requesting relief from the stay "has the burden of proof on the issue of the debtor's equity in property; and the party opposing such relief has the burden of proof on all other issues." Bankruptcy Code § 362(g).

b. Turnover of Collateral by Secured Party

Bankruptcy Code § 542(a) basically requires the turnover of the property of the debtor's estate to the trustee. This means that a secured party in possession, whether by original pledge or by repossession under 1999 § 9-609, must deliver the collateral to the trustee, unless excused by the court. This is so, even if the security interest has been perfected and is immune from attack under the Bankruptcy Code, although such a perfected interest ordinarily retains that status under the Bankruptcy Code. In some instances, particularly in a Chapter 7 case, the secured party in possession may be permitted to retain possession.

c. Abandonment by the Trustee

The trustee is permitted, after notice and a hearing, to "abandon any property of the estate that is burdensome to the estate or that is of inconsequential value and benefit to the estate." Bankruptcy Code § 554(a). The court may also order abandonment at the request "of a party in interest." Bankruptcy Code § 554(b). This should permit abandonment by the trustee of collateral that is valued at less than the secured debt and allow the secured party to take and dispose of such collateral under 1999 § 9-601 et seq. The provisions for abandonment are in addition to the provision for relief from the automatic stay, discussed in § 3a of this chapter of the Nutshell.

d. Sale or Disposition of Collateral

Bankruptcy Code § 363 provides for sale of the collateral by the trustee. In most instances, the sale must either be authorized by the secured party or authorized by the bankruptcy court. Provision is made for "adequate protection" of the interest of the secured party when the trustee sells the collateral (see discussion of "adequate protection" in § 3a of this chapter of the Nutshell). In most instances, the sale is free and clear of the security interest or any other interest; but the "adequate protection" given the secured party substitutes for the collateral now sold. Bankruptcy Code § 363 also authorizes use or lease of the collateral by the estate.

In certain instances, a trustee may borrow on the collateral on behalf of the debtor's estate. Although a lender to the trustee will generally occupy a status inferior to that of a secured party with a perfected interest in the collateral, Bankruptcy Code § 364(d) permits borrowing by the trustee and the granting to the new lender of superpriority over the secured party with respect to the collateral. However, where such superpriority is allowed, there must be "adequate protection" to the secured party. (See discussion of "adequate protection" in § 3a of this chapter of the Nutshell.)

Generally, borrowing will take place only where the trustee (or debtor in possession) continues to operate the debtor's business, and such borrowing must be approved by the bankruptcy court. This will normally occur in a Chapter 11 proceeding, and is rather unlikely in a Chapter 7 or Chapter 13 proceeding.

e. *Status of Secured Party*

Bankruptcy Code § 506 deals with the determination of secured status. The court may allow a claim "secured by a lien on property in which the estate has an interest." Where the secured party is unable to obtain relief from an automatic stay (see § 3a of this chapter of the Nutshell) or obtain abandonment of the collateral (see § 3c of this chapter of the Nutshell), it is often necessary for the secured party to participate in the bankruptcy case.

If the value of the collateral exceeds the secured debt, the secured party may claim in that status, assuming that the security interest was perfected prior to the debtor's bankruptcy and is not subject to attack as a preference or otherwise. The secured party is entitled after the sale of the collateral under Bankruptcy Code § 363 to full payment of the secured debt, plus interest, together with reasonable fees, costs or charges provided by the security agreement or other agreement. See Bankruptcy Code § 506(b). However, the trustee may also recover from the proceeds of the sale "reasonable, necessary costs and expenses of preserving, or disposing of, such property to the extent of any benefit" to the secured party. Bankruptcy Code § 506(c).

If the collateral is valued at less than the debt secured, the secured party may file proof of claim as an unsecured claimant to the extent of the debt exceeding the value of the collateral. Bankruptcy Code § 506(a). It should be noted that Bankruptcy Code §§ 501 and 502 cover the filing and allowance of claims generally against the debtor's estate.

It also should be noted that even though a bankruptcy discharges the debt, i.e. the debtor's personal liability is terminated, the lien resulting from the security interest is not so affected.

f. Unenforceable Security Interest

A security interest that is unenforceable against the debtor is equally unenforceable against the debtor's estate. This is made clear by Bankruptcy Code § 558, which gives the debtor's estate the benefit of any defense available to the debtor against a third person, "including statutes of limitations, statutes of frauds, usury, and other personal defenses." A waiver by the debtor after commencement of the case is ineffective.

This means that a security interest which does not attach under 1999 § 9-203(b) is not enforceable in bankruptcy. As to the requirements of a writing or possession and other requirements for attachment, see Chapter 2 and Chapter 3, § 1 of this Nutshell.

Moreover, Bankruptcy Code § 558 should enable

the trustee to set aside a secured transaction for any other reason that would have enabled the debtor to get out of the deal, such as unconscionability where applicable to a credit sale of goods under Uniform Commercial Code § 2-302, fraud, duress, undue influence, mutual mistake, or any defense available under a consumer-protective statute.

§ 4. The "Strong-Arm" Provision of the Bankruptcy Code

Bankruptcy Code § 544(a), like its predecessor of the 1898 Act, might sometimes (perhaps with some exaggeration) be referred to as the "strong-arm" clause. *It basically allows the trustee to set aside an unperfected security interest* and relegate the unperfected secured party to general unsecured claimant status. Thus, the collateral would now be sold and the proceeds applied to all unsecured claims, as opposed to being used to satisfy exclusively the unperfected secured party's claim. Bankruptcy Code § 544(a) enables the trustee to avoid any transfer of property that is voidable by (1) a creditor who obtains a judicial lien on the collateral, (2) a creditor who extends credit and then obtains an unsatisfied execution lien on the collateral, and (3) a bona fide purchaser of real property other than fixtures from the debtor against whom applicable law permits such transfer to be perfected.

The first two rules above are similar to rules of the 1898 Act. The latter rule (referring to a bona fide purchaser of real property) was not in the 1898 Act. Whether the strong-arm clause could also apply to set aside a security interest in a fixture which was perfected by a means other than by a fixture filing (see Chapter 7, § 7 of this Nutshell) was none too clear prior to the 1984 amendments to the Bankruptcy Code. The 1984 amendments clarify the rules as to fixtures and would give priority to a security interest in a fixture perfected by any means prior to bankruptcy.

It is important to note that the trustee is given the status of an ideal judgment creditor, execution creditor or real estate purchaser. Moreover, the "strong-arm" clause applies whether or not a judgment creditor, lien creditor or real estate purchaser actually exists. As such a creditor or real estate purchaser, the trustee may defeat the holder of a security interest which is unperfected at the time of filing of the petition.

The "strong-arm" clause is given full recognition in 1999 §§ 9-317(a)(2), 9-102(a)(52) of the Uniform Commercial Code, which makes a security interest subordinate to the rights of a person who becomes a lien creditor before the security interest is perfected, and which explicitly recognizes a trustee in bankruptcy as such a lien creditor as of the date of filing of the petition. In other words, the trustee not only succeeds to the debtor's rights in the collateral, but is "promoted" to the status of a lien creditor and a bona fide purchaser of real property, even though the creditors represented are general creditors without a lien.

Although the trustee as a lien creditor under the "strong-arm" clause has priority over the rights of a secured party with an unperfected interest, the "strong-arm" clause has no application where the security interest is perfected before the time of bankruptcy (when the petition is filed), even if perfected only hours before bankruptcy. Note, however, that the trustee in bankruptcy is also armed with certain other legal weapons which may be used to defeat even a perfected security interest. See §§ 5 and 6 of this chapter of the Nutshell. See also § 3a of this chapter in this Nutshell that indicates a post-petition filing is allowed in some circumstances.

Example 1. Secured Party took a security interest in certain equipment purchased by Debtor on February 1. Debtor went bankrupt (the petition was filed) on November 1. Secured Party filed and thereby perfected its security interest on November 2. The trustee in bankruptcy avoids the security interest and takes the equipment under the "strong-arm" clause.

Example 2.   Secured Party took a security interest in certain equipment purchased by Debtor on February 1.   Secured Party filed and thereby perfected its security interest on October 31. Debtor went bankrupt (the petition was filed) on November 1. The trustee in bankruptcy may not avoid the security interest and take the collateral under the "strong-arm" clause (though they might have other grounds for attacking the security interest).

Note: The same result obtains in Example 2 if Secured Party, instead of filing, had taken possession of the collateral on October 31. Repossession of the collateral perfects an otherwise unperfected security interest as it operates like a pledge. See Chapter 4, § 4a of this Nutshell.

§ 5.   Preferential Transfers

a. The General Rule

Common law and the law of most states permit an insolvent debtor to treat some creditors more favorably than other creditors by paying the preferred creditors to the exclusion of the others. [However, some states have enacted the Uniform

Fraudulent Transfers Act which at § 5(b) makes some types of preferences avoidable.] Moreover, a diligent creditor may obtain more favorable status against an insolvent debtor by getting a judgment or execution lien on property of the debtor under state law. On the other hand, federal bankruptcy law takes a different position as to preferential payments or voluntary or involuntary transfers by an insolvent debtor to certain favored creditors. The Bankruptcy Code permits a bankruptcy trustee to set aside so-called "preferential transfers" made within a relatively short time before the debtor's bankruptcy.

Under Bankruptcy Code § 547(b), five conditions must be met in order that a trustee may strike down a voluntary or involuntary transfer of property of an insolvent debtor to a particular creditor. The transfer of the debtor's property must be:

(1) to or for the benefit of a creditor;

(2) for or on account of an antecedent debt owed by the debtor before such transfer was made;

(3) made while the debtor was insolvent (it should be noted that Bankruptcy Code § 547(f) adds a rebuttable presumption that the debtor has been insolvent during the 90 days preceding the filing of the petition);

(4) made within 90 days before the filing of the

petition (but a special one-year rule discussed below in § 5b of this chapter of the Nutshell governs a transfer to an "insider");

(5) a transfer that enables the creditor to receive more than they would have received had the transfer not been made and there had been a distribution to that creditor in a liquidation proceeding under Bankruptcy Code Chapter 7.

The Bankruptcy Code provision will apply to a secured transaction *if perfection is delayed and takes place within the 90-day period.* In general, Bankruptcy Code § 547(e) has the effect of fixing the time of transfer at the time of perfection of a security interest, rather than at an earlier time of attachment of the security interest. However, perfection within 30 days of attachment is deemed to relate back to the time of attachment. If the debt owed the secured creditor was incurred at that time, the transfer was not on account of an antecedent debt and is not avoidable as a preference. See Bankruptcy Code § 547(e)(2).

Example 1. On April 1, Debtor purchased and took delivery of widgets on credit and gave Seller a security interest for the unpaid price of $10,000. Seller filed a financing statement on May 15. Debtor filed a bankruptcy petition on August 1 (within 90 days of May 15). The delayed perfection by Seller can be set aside as a preferential transfer. Note, however, that if the widgets are consumer goods within the Code rule on perfection upon attachment alone (see Chapter 4, § 2a of this Nutshell), the filing on May 15 is not a preferential transfer.

Example 2. Assume the facts of Example 1 above, except that Seller, instead of filing, repossessed the collateral on May 15. The delayed perfection by repossession can be set aside as a preferential transfer if the widgets are not consumer goods.

Example 3. Assume the facts of Example 1 above, except that the bankruptcy petition was filed on September 1. Since perfection, although delayed, took place more than 90 days before the filing of the petition, there is no preferential transfer unless the secured party, Seller, is an "insider" (see discussion of the "insider" rules in § 5b of this chapter of the Nutshell).

Example 4. Assume that the credit purchase of Example 1 took place on April 1, the filing was on April 10 and the bankruptcy petition was filed on July 6. Since perfection, although within 90 days of the filing of the petition, was within 30 days after attachment of the security interest, there is no preferential transfer because the transfer is deemed to have occurred when the security interest attached at which time the debtor incurred the debt owed the secured party. Thus, the transfer was not on account of an antecedent debt and is not avoidable as a preference.

b. "Insider" Transfers

Special rules govern a preferential transfer to an "insider." The term "insider" has a lengthy definition in Bankruptcy Code § 101(31), which includes a number of personal or business relationship categories between the debtor and the creditor receiving the transfer. Among such "insider" categories of creditors are certain close relatives of an individual debtor, officers, directors or persons in control of a corporate debtor, or partners of a partnership debtor.

Where a transfer is made to an "insider," the transfer may be set aside not only within 90 days, as discussed above, but also between 90 days and one year before the date of filing of the petition.

"Insider" problems should not affect most secured transactions where problems of preferential transfer exist. But an "insider" problem might arise where there is a relationship between the debtor and secured party falling within the Bankruptcy Code §

101(31) definition. Thus, delayed perfection taking place more than 90 days but less than one year before the filing of a bankruptcy petition might be upset if the secured party is an "insider." A possible example of an "insider" secured party might include a controlling stockholder of a corporate debtor or a financer who has taken over the management of the debtor's business.

Although the possible time of the preferential transfer is extended where the creditor is an "insider," the rebuttable presumption of insolvency runs for but 90 days before the filing of the petition.

c. Exceptions to the "Preference" Rules

Nine exceptions to the basic "preferential transfer" rules of Bankruptcy Code § 547(b) are listed in Bankruptcy Code § 547(c):

(1) A "substantially contemporaneous" exchange for new value given to the debtor. This will protect cash sales where the seller is paid by check and waits several days to deposit and collect it. Similarly protected is a security interest for new value taken and promptly perfected.

(2) Ordinary-course payments of debts. This permits routine bill payments and should protect

most sellers on open trade terms who are paid within a reasonable time after any sale.

(3) Purchase-money security interests which are perfected within 30 days after the debtor received possession of the collateral.

(4) Advances made by a creditor after a preferential transfer takes place. For example, if a debtor gives a creditor a security interest in certain collateral to secure an antecedent debt of $10,000, the security interest is delayed in perfection which takes place within 90 days of bankruptcy, but if the creditor then advances an additional $5,000, the amount of preferential transfer would be the value of the security interest less the $5,000.

(5) Certain perfected security interests covering after-acquired property. See the discussion that follows in § 5d of this chapter of the Nutshell.

(6) Statutory liens that may not be avoided under Bankruptcy Code § 545. This should not affect a security interest, which is a consensual lien and not a statutory lien.

(7) Bona fide payments made to a spouse or child of a debtor in connection with a separation agreement or divorce decree. This exception should not affect a security interest.

(8) Regarding consumer debtors, where the aggregate value of the property transferred is less than $600, such a transfer will not be avoided as a preference. Thus, acquisition of a security interest in property of a value less than $600 to secure a consumer debt would not be voidable as a preference.

(9) Regarding nonconsumer debtors, where the aggregate value of the property transferred is less that $5,000, such a transfer will not be avoided as a preference. Thus, acquisition of a security interest in property of a value less that $5,000 to secure a nonconsumer debt would not be voidable as a preference.

d. *Where Security Interest Covers After-Acquired Property*

Probably the most troublesome area of litigation involving the effect of the 1898 Act on a Uniform Commercial Code security interest was an effort to apply the "preference" provisions of the 1898 Act to a security interest covering not only property then owned by the debtor but also property subsequently acquired. Generally, as to after-acquired property as collateral, see Chapter 2, § 6b of this Nutshell. Such "floating liens" are frequently used in financing inventory or accounts which normally "turn over" in the ordinary course of the debtor's business. Under 1999 § 9-204(a), a security agreement may provide that after-acquired property (except for consumer goods in most instances) will serve as security for the debtor's obligations. Moreover, under 1999 § 9-205, the security agreement may give the debtor the power to use or dispose of the collateral at will, without accounting to the secured party. Thus, if a security agreement covering inventory or accounts contains an after-acquired property clause and is properly perfected, the debtor may use the collateral as business needs dictate.

In some instances under the 1898 Act, a trustee in bankruptcy sought to set aside as a preferential transfer security interests in property acquired by the debtor within four months of bankruptcy (the preference period under the 1898 Act) under a security agreement covering after-acquired property, where filing took place more than four months before bankruptcy. The trustee would have argued that the time a "transfer" occurred was at the time the security interest was perfected, and that the security interest in after-acquired collateral was perfected only when the debtor acquired rights in the collateral, as prior to when the security interest was unattached. Thus the trustee would have argued the "transfer" occurred when the debtor acquired the after-acquired collateral and that the transfer was on account of an antecedent debt, the loan to the debtor having been made previously. The 1898 Act had no clear provision addressed to this problem, but most decided cases rejected the trustee's argument and upheld the security interest covering the after-acquired collateral, as against a claim of preferential transfer.

The Bankruptcy Code in § 547(c)(5) attempts a statutory solution by declaring in effect that a perfected security interest "in inventory or a receivable or the proceeds of either" is subject to attack as a preference to the extent that the secured party improves their position during the 90-day (or one-year in the case of the "insider") period preceding the filing of the petition "to the prejudice of other creditors holding unsecured claims."

Two measuring points are used: 90 days before the petition is filed and the date of the filing of the petition. Where the "insider" rule applies, the measuring points are one year before the filing of the petition and the date of filing. (An alternative rule substituting the date on which "new value was first given" for either the 90-day or one year date applies if new value is first given after such 90-day or one-year date.) In essence, if the secured party has improved their position with respect to the value of the collateral as against the secured debt at the time the petition is filed over the earlier measuring date (usually 90 days), the extent of improvement may be attacked as a preferential transfer.

Example. Debtor files a bankruptcy petition on May 1. Creditor has a valid security interest and floating lien on Debtor's inventory, entered into 15 months earlier at which time Creditor filed a financing statement proper in all respects. 90 days before May 1, the inventory had a value of $90,000 but the debt was $150,000. On May 1, the changing inventory had a value of $110,000 but the debt was $120,000. The debt in excess of the collateral was $60,000 90 days before May 1, but was only $10,000 on May 1. Thus, $50,000 of the interest in the inventory is a preferential transfer, and the secured party may claim only $60,000 of the $110,000 value of inventory at the time of bankruptcy.

It should be noted that Bankruptcy Code § 547(c)(5) only speaks in terms of "inventory or a receivable or the proceeds of either." Thus, a security interest in after-acquired equipment acquired within 90 days of the filing of the petition would likely be subject to attack as a preferential transfer.

In short, the secured party with a perfected security interest covering after-acquired property is often not in as good a position under the Bankruptcy Code as under case law arising under the 1898 Act.

It should be noted that a security interest covering after-acquired property is generally limited as to property acquired by the debtor or the estate after bankruptcy. See § 7 of this chapter of the Nutshell.

§ 6.   Fraudulent Transfers

Bankruptcy Code § 548 permits the trustee to set aside any transfer by, or obligation incurred by, the debtor within two years before the filing of the petition, if the transfer or obligation was intended to hinder, delay or defraud any creditor, or if less than reasonably equivalent value was received and the debtor was insolvent or became insolvent as a result of the transfer or obligation, or where certain other like circumstances exist. This Bankruptcy Code provision is based on the Uniform Fraudulent Transfer Act.

Although fraudulent transfer problems should rarely exist in connection with secured transactions, it is conceivable that a security interest might be attacked under Bankruptcy Code § 548 if it is taken for grossly inadequate consideration or otherwise taken with intent to hinder, delay or defraud other creditors. As is the case with Bankruptcy Code

§ 547 preferences, a transfer is deemed to occur when it is perfected. See, Bankruptcy Code § 548(d).

State fraudulent transfer laws might also be utilized under Bankruptcy Code § 544(b) which permits the trustee to "avoid any transfer of an interest of the debtor in property or any obligation incurred by the debtor that is voidable under applicable law by a creditor holding an unsecured claim that is allowable....." Thus, if an unsecured creditor could avoid a transfer by the debtor, the trustee may step into the shoes of that creditor and completely avoid the transfer.

Bankruptcy Code § 544(b) should rarely apply in a secured transaction situation except to attack the acquisition of a security interest as a fraudulent conveyance. The reason is that it permits the trustee to act only if an *unsecured creditor* could act. Thus, the trustee could not step into the shoes of a creditor with a lien superior to a security interest, where there is delayed perfection.

Example. On February 1, Debtor gave Secured Party a security interest in widgets for a debt of $5,000. On March 1, Creditor levied on the widgets for an unsatisfied judgment of $100. On April 1, Secured Party filed a financing statement. On October 1, Debtor filed a bankruptcy petition. The trustee may not attack the security interest under Bankruptcy Code § 544(b) because Creditor had a lien and was not an unsecured creditor.

Probably the only possible application of Bankruptcy Code § 544(b) to set aside a security interest might be where an unsecured creditor could set the interest aside as a fraudulent transfer under state law. Note that the trustee could utilize Bankruptcy Code § 544(b) to attack a fraudulent transfer not subject to attack under Bankruptcy Code § 548 because it took place more than two years prior to bankruptcy.

§ 7.   Property Acquired After Bankruptcy

Problems of preferential transfers affecting after-acquired property are discussed above (§ 5d of this chapter of the Nutshell). In addition, the rights of a secured party to certain after-acquired collateral of a debtor are further restricted under Bankruptcy Code § 552. A security interest is ineffective with respect to property acquired by the estate or by the debtor after the commencement of the case, even though a security agreement entered into before the commencement of the case covers such property. See Bankruptcy Code § 552(a).

There is an exception to the above exclusionary rule. Proceeds, products, offspring, rents or profits from property subject to a perfected security interest, received after the commencement of the case, may be subject to the security interest if the security agreement extends to such property. However, the court "after notice and a hearing and based on the equities of the case" may order otherwise. See Bankruptcy Code § 552(b). Thus, if inventory subject to a perfected security interest is sold by the debtor prior to the filing of the petition and payment is received after such filing, the payment as proceeds would ordinarily go to the secured party.

§ 8. Security Interest in Exempt Property

Certain property of a debtor is exempt and is not distributed to creditors. Under Bankruptcy Code § 522, an individual debtor is entitled to claim exemptions allowed under state law or, alternatively, to take certain specified Bankruptcy Code exemptions. A state by legislation may limit the debtor to "state law" exemptions, which has occurred in many states.

Usually, a security interest which is otherwise valid in bankruptcy applies to exempt property to the extent permitted by state law. But certain security interests in exempt property are invalidated in bankruptcy. Bankruptcy Code § 522(f) permits the debtor to avoid a "nonpossessory, nonpurchase-money security interest" in various described household or similar consumer goods, implements or tools of the trade or health aids. Moreover, Bankruptcy Code § 522(e) makes ineffective a waiver by the debtor of the right to avoid such a nonpossessory and nonpurchase-money security interest.

A right of the debtor to redeem exempt property from a security interest is also given in Bankruptcy Code § 722. An individual debtor whose estate is in liquidation under Bankruptcy Code Chapter 7 may redeem "tangible personal property intended primarily for personal, family or household use from a lien securing a dischargeable consumer debt," if such property is exempted under Bankruptcy Code § 522 or has been abandoned by the trustee under Bankruptcy Code § 554, "by paying the holder of the secured claim the amount of the secured claim of such holder that is secured by such lien." The allowed secured claim is equal to the amount of the debt or value of the collateral, whichever is less. This rule applies whether or not the debtor has waived the right of redemption. See Bankruptcy Code § 722.

Example. Debtor, prior to filing bankruptcy, granted Creditor a UCC Article 9 purchase-money security interest in household furniture that is exempt under Bankruptcy Code § 522. Debtor files bankruptcy and owes creditor $5,000. The furniture has a value of $100. Debtor may redeem the furniture by payment of $100. To redeem outside of bankruptcy, the full amount of the debt must be paid. See Chapter 9, § 9 of this Nutshell and1999 § 9-623.

§ 9. Reclamation Rights of Unpaid Sellers

Priorities affecting an unpaid seller of goods and a secured party with a security interest in such goods given by the buyer are discussed in Chapter 7, § 5 of this Nutshell. However, the right of an unpaid seller in a cash sale under Uniform Commercial Code § 2-507(2) or § 2-511(3) or an unpaid seller in a credit sale under § 2-702(2) and (3) to reclaim when the buyer becomes bankrupt was somewhat questionable in case law under the 1898 Act.

Bankruptcy Code § 546 has the effect of permitting a limited right of reclamation by an unpaid seller. The seller has to make a written demand for reclamation "not later than 45 days after the date of receipt of such goods by the debtor." If, however, the 45-day period expires after the commencement of the bankruptcy case, the seller has 20 days after the date of commencement to make the reclamation claim. By contrast, note that under UCC § 2-702(2) the seller's right of reclamation arises when the seller discovers the buyer has received goods on credit while insolvent; the seller must then make demand for the goods within 10 days after receipt, although that 10-day deadline is inapplicable if the buyer has misrepresented their solvency in writing within 3 months before delivery.

It should be noted that Bankruptcy Code § 546(c) permits reclamation by the unpaid seller within the 45-day period both in a "cash sale" situation under Code §§ 2-507(2) and 2-511(3) and in a "credit sale" situation under Code § 2-702(2). But the § 2-702(2) language doing away with the 10-day limitation when there is a written misrepresentation of solvency by the buyer does not apply in a proceeding under the Bankruptcy Code. In other words, the unpaid seller has to make a written demand for the goods within 45 days of receipt by the buyer.

CHAPTER 9

DEFAULT AND ENFORCEMENT
OF SECURITY INTEREST

§ 1. What Constitutes Default

UCC Article 9 has no provision defining the term "default" or specifying what constitutes a "default." Thus, contract law generally governs the issue of whether a default has occurred. See pre-revision UCC § 1-103 and revised § 1-103(b). From this, it follows that a breach by the debtor of any of the terms of the security agreement will constitute a default. The most typical default is failure to make a payment when due, but the security agreement may, and often does, specify acts on the part of the debtor other than nonpayment which are also events of default. For a discussion of events of default in a security agreement, see Chapter 2, § 7e.

Security agreements frequently also provide that upon the occurrence of an event of default, the secured party may accelerate payment. Sometimes, a security agreement may even permit acceleration at will, or when the secured party deems itself to be insecure. When acceleration takes place, failure of the debtor to make the total of all payments due will be a default. For a discussion of acceleration clauses in a security agreement, see Chapter 2, § 6d. It should be noted that consumer protection legislation and regulatory law separate from UCC Article 9 may prohibit acceleration under some circumstances.

Upon the happening of one or more events of default specified in the security agreement, the secured party may resort to the "default" provisions of Article 9 (1999 §§ 9-601 through 9-628). However, the secured party may not take "default" action in the absence of an event of default set forth in the security agreement. The taking of such "default" action in the absence of default may subject the secured party to possible liability to the debtor.

Example. Debtor gave Creditor a security interest in their inventory to secure a debt calling for monthly payments. Immediately after making a monthly payment, Debtor died. No payments were in arrears at that time and no other event of default had occurred. The security agreement had no provision making Debtor's death an event of default. Nevertheless, Creditor takes immediate action to repossess the collateral. The repossession is improper and Creditor may be held liable to Debtor's executor, administrator or heirs for losses sustained upon such repossession, and possibly also for punitive damages.

Note: It should be kept in mind that the rights of the secured party upon default by the debtor are limited where the debtor is in a bankruptcy under federal law. See Chapter 8 for general discussion of the effect of bankruptcy.

The 1999 Code has a special provision regarding default in connection with an agricultural lien. For a definition of "agricultural lien," see 1999 § 9-102(a)(5). Agricultural liens fall within the scope of the 1999 Code. 1999 § 9-109(a)(2). A default occurs in connection with an agricultural lien at the time the secured party becomes entitled to enforce the lien in accordance with the statute under which the lien was created. 1999 § 9-606. Once such a default occurs, the holder of the agricultural lien has available the enforcement remedies of a secured party generally. See Comment 2 to 1999 § 9-606.

Even when a default occurs, the secured party cannot enforce the security interest when the secured party waives the right to do so. A "waiver" occurs when the secured party knowingly relinquishes their right to enforce a security interest. For example, according to some case law, if the debtor has failed repeatedly to make timely payments contrary to the terms of a security agreement, or has repeatedly sold collateral contrary to the terms of a security agreement, without objection of the secured party, the right to enforce the security agreement upon recurrence of such events of default may have been waived. Under such circumstances, to reinstate the secured party's right to enforce the security interest in the event of waiver, the secured party must notify the debtor that in the future strict compliance with the terms of the security agreement will be required.

§ 2.   Rights of Secured Party Generally

When the debtor is in default, the rights and obligations of the secured party and the rights of the debtor are set forth in Part 6 of 1999 Article 9, §§ 9-601 through 9-628. The rights of the secured party in the collateral after the debtor's default are of the essence of a secured transaction. They are the rights which distinguish the secured from the unsecured lender.

The secured party is given a broad choice of legal weapons with which to enforce their rights. These are somewhat indexed in 1999 § 9-601(a). In this regard, the secured party has the rights and remedies provided in 1999 §§ 9-601 through 9-628 and (with some limitations which may not be waived at least before default) the rights provided in the security agreement.   Under 1999 § 9-601(a), the secured party also has the following rights:

(1) to reduce their claim to judgment;

(2) to foreclose or otherwise enforce the security interest by any available judicial procedure;

(3) if the collateral is documents, to proceed either as to the documents or as to the goods they cover.

When the secured party is in possession, they have all the rights, remedies and duties prescribed in 1999 § 9-207.   See 1999 § 9-601(b).   As to such rights and duties, see Chapter 3, § 4.

The above rights and remedies are stated to be cumulative.   1999 § 9-601(c).   In other words, the secured party may elect one of the above courses of action without being barred from taking some other course in order to enforce the security interest.   For example, the secured party may obtain a judgment for the amount of the debt and then attempt to collect it by any legal means (such as by execution on other property of the debtor, by garnishment of a debt due the debtor from a third person or by pursuing other creditor's remedies).   Such action does not prevent the secured party from realizing on the collateral under the "default" procedures of Article 9.

Certain rights are also given the secured party under the other "default" provisions of Article 9. These are summarized here and discussed in detail in later sections of this chapter. Among such rights are:

(1) the right to repossess the collateral, under 1999 § 9-609;

(2) the right to make direct collection from any account debtor or obligor on an instrument and to take control of any proceeds to which the secured party is entitled, under 1999 §§ 9-607, 9-608.

(3) the right to sell or otherwise dispose of the collateral, under 1999 §§ 9-610, 9-611, 9-615, 9-617, 9-618 and 9-624;

(4) the right to propose to take the collateral in satisfaction of the debt (the right of strict foreclosure), under circumstances outlined at 1999 §§ 9-620 through 9-622, 9-624.

When the security agreement covers both real and personal property, the secured party may proceed under the default procedures of Article 9 with respect to the personal property or may proceed exclusively under real estate law with respect to both real and personal property. See 1999 § 9-604.

§ 3.   Judicial Foreclosure and Sale

Upon default, the secured party may reduce their claim to judgment, foreclose or otherwise enforce the security interest by any judicial procedure. 1999 § 9-601(a)(1). Note that under the 1999 Code agricultural liens can be enforced in the same manner. While in probably the majority of instances, the secured party will repossess the collateral and sell it without resort to judicial process, there may be instances when it may be desirable to utilize the courts, obtain a judgment against the debtor and execute on the debtor's property, including the collateral securing the debt. In such a case, under 1999 § 9-601(e) the lien relates back to the earliest of the date of perfection of the security interest or agricultural lien, the date of filing a financing statement, or any date specified in a statute under which the agricultural lien was created.

In other words, if it is necessary for the secured party to execute on the collateral, but the security interest was earlier perfected by a still-effective filing, the time of execution relates back to the time of filing. Thus, if the debtor becomes bankrupt within 90 days of the time of execution, but if filing took place more than 90 days before bankruptcy, the trustee cannot attack the execution as a preferential transfer under the Bankruptcy Code. See Chapter 8,

§ 5 for discussion of preferential transfers.

Where the collateral is sold by a judicial sale following execution, this is considered a foreclosure of the security interest by judicial procedure. The secured party is permitted to purchase the collateral at such a judicial sale and hold it free of other requirements of Article 9. See 1999 § 9-601(f).

Moreover, where there is a sale approved in a judicial proceeding, the sale is conclusively deemed to have been commercially reasonable. See 1999 § 9-627(c). However, this does not mean that a judicial sale is necessary or that a nonjudicial sale is necessarily commercially unreasonable.

§ 4.   Debtor's Protective Rights

After default, the debtor has the rights and remedies provided in the "default" provisions of 1999 Article 9 §§ 9-601 through 9-628, those provided in the security agreement, and those provided in 1999 § 9-207 dealing with rights and duties when the secured party has possession. See 1999 § 9-601(d). It should be noted that1999 § 9-207 applies not only to the situation where the secured party is in possession before default as a pledgee, but also where the secured party is in possession after default. Nevertheless, the relations of the parties have been changed under default and 1999 § 9-207 must be read together with the default provisions of Article 9. In particular, agreements permitted under 1999 § 9-207 cannot waive or modify certain rights of the debtor following default. See Comment 4 to 1999 § 9-607. As to rights and duties when the secured party is in possession, see Chapter 3, § 4.

1999 § 9-602 sets forth certain rights of the debtor following default which may not be waived or varied by agreement (i.e., the security agreement) except as permitted by 1999 § 9-624. The rights that are listed as non-waiveable prior to default under the 1999 Code include the following:

(1) Rights under 1999 § 9-207(b)(4)(C), which deals with use and operation of the collateral by the secured party.

(2) Rights under 1999 § 9-210, which deals with requests for an accounting and requests concerning a list of collateral and statement of account.

(3) Rights under 1999 § 9-607(c) which deals with collection and enforcement of collateral.

(4) Rights under 1999 §§ 9-608(a) and 9-615(c) to the extent that they deal with application or payment of noncash proceeds of collection, enforcement, or disposition.

(5) Rights under 1999 §§ 9-608(a) and 9-615(d) to the extent that they require accounting for or payment of surplus proceeds of collateral.

(6) Rights under 1999 § 9-609 to the extent that it imposes upon a secured party that takes possession of collateral without judicial process the duty to do so without breach of the peace.

(7) Rights under 1999 §§ 9-610(b), 9-611, 9-613, and 9-614, which deal with disposition of collateral.

(8) Rights under 1999 § 9-615(f), which deals with calculation of a deficiency or surplus when a disposition is made to the secured party, a person related to the secured party, or a secondary obligor.

(9) Rights under 1999 § 9-616, which deals with explanation of the calculation of a surplus or deficiency.

(10) Rights under 1999 §§ 9-620, 9-621, 9-622, which deal with acceptance of collateral in satisfaction of obligation.

(11) Rights under 1999 § 9-623, which deals with redemption of collateral.

(12) Rights under 1999 § 9-624, which deals with permissible waivers.

(13)   Rights under §§ 9-625 and 9-626, which deal with the secured party's liability for failure to comply with this article.

Under the 1999 Code, certain debtor rights are waiveable by an agreement entered into and authenticated after default. 1999 § 9-624. Those rights include the right to notification of disposition of collateral under 1999 § 9-611, the right to require disposition of collateral under 1999 § 9-620(e), and except in consumer transactions, the right to redeem collateral under 1999 § 9-623.

The reason for not permitting waiver of the foregoing rules in the security agreement or otherwise before default was explained in Comment 4 to 1972 § 9-501. That Comment states in part:

"In the area of rights after default our legal system has traditionally looked with suspicion on agreements designed to cut down the debtor's rights and free the secured party of their duties: no mortgage clause has ever been allowed to clog the equity of redemption. The default situation offers great scope for overreaching; the suspicious attitude of the courts has been grounded in common sense."

Although there is no such Comment to the 1999 Code, it is clear the same policy sentiment underlies the non-waiver provisions of the 1999 Code above described.

However, 1999 § 9-603 does permit the parties by agreement to determine the standards by which the fulfillment of these rights and duties are to be measured if such standards are not manifestly unreasonable. See also the similar provision of pre-revision § 1-102(3) and revised § 1-302(a).   For example, the security agreement might conceivably contain some provision relating to the method of disposition of the collateral after default, such as the place of sale, if such provision is not "manifestly unreasonable."   On the other hand, the 1999 Code invalidates such agreements to the extent they relate to the duty not to breach the peace when a secured party repossesses collateral extrajudicially.   1999 § 9-603(b).

CAVEAT.   While Article 9 generally permits waiver by the debtor of their rights after default, statutes outside the Code such as consumer credit laws and retail installment sales laws may contain more restrictive provisions relating to consumer goods as collateral than those in Article 9.   Such other statutes control in the event of conflict with Article 9.

§ 5.   Collection Rights for Accounts, Instruments or Chattel Paper

a. Generally

The secured party is entitled to notify an account debtor (the person who is obligated on an account, chattel paper or general intangible) or the obligor of an instrument (such as the maker of a promissory note taken as collateral for an obligation of the payee) to make payment to them (the secured party). This may be done whether or not the assignor (debtor) was previously making their own collections on the collateral.   See 1999 § 9-607(a)(1).

Example. Seller-Assignor sells goods on open account to various account debtors. Seller-Assignor assigns the accounts to Secured Party. The assignments are on a "non-notification" basis permitting Seller-Assignor to make their own collections from the account debtors (permitted under 1999 § 9-205). Upon default by Seller-Assignor, Secured Party notifies account debtors to make payments to them (Secured Party). Account debtors must thereafter pay Secured Party as assignee under 1999 § 9-406(a).

The secured party is also entitled to take control of any proceeds to which they are entitled under

1999 § 9-315. See 1999 § 9-607(a).

b. *Duties of Secured Party; Right to Surplus or Liability for Deficiency*

In some instances, a secured party taking an assignment of an account, chattel paper or general intangible or taking a note or other instrument as security may be entitled to charge back uncollected collateral against the debtor-assignor or may be otherwise entitled to full or limited recourse against the debtor-assignor. In such a case, 1999 § 9-607(c) requires that the secured party proceed in a commercially reasonable manner in making the collection, but they are entitled to deduct their reasonable expenses of realization from the collection. If the security agreement secures an indebtedness, the secured party must account to the debtor-assignor for any surplus and, unless otherwise agreed, the debtor-assignor is liable for any deficiency.

This means that where the assignee does not assume the full credit risk and retains a right of full or limited recourse or charge back for uncollectible accounts, both the debtor-assignor and other creditors have a right that the assignee not "dump the accounts" if the result will be to increase a possible deficiency claim or to reduce a possible surplus. In other words, the assignee must liquidate the accounts in a commercially reasonable manner. See Comment 9 to 1999 § 9-607.

On the other hand, if the underlying transaction is a sale of accounts or chattel paper [which is within Article 9 under 1999 § 9-109(a)(3)] and there is no right of recourse or charge back if the account or chattel paper is uncollectible, the assignee assumes the credit risk completely. In such circumstances, the debtor is not entitled to any surplus, and nor are they liable for any deficiency, unless the security agreement so provides. See 1999 § 9-608(b) and Comment 3.

§ 6. Secured Party's Right of Repossession

a. Generally

Unless otherwise agreed a secured party has on default the right to take possession of the collateral. In taking possession, a secured party may proceed without judicial process if this can be done without breach of the peace. 1999 § 9-609(a), (b). Those Code provisions also permit the secured party to proceed by "action" to take possession of the collateral. Presumably, this would permit repossession by replevin or a claim and delivery action.

These provisions permit "peaceable" self-help repossession by the secured party without having to resort to the courts. A number of decisions have considered whether or not self-help repossession is peaceable under particular circumstances; in this connection, pre-Code decisions are also on point. Generally, courts define a "breach of the peace" to be a disturbance of public order by an act of violence, or by any act likely to produce violence, or which by causing consternation and alarm disturbs the peace and quiet of the community. While an exhaustive list of circumstances involving "peaceable" repossession or repossession constituting a "breach of the peace" is beyond the scope of this Nutshell, a few rules may be set forth here.

The following acts are likely to be considered as "peaceable" in connection with repossession.

(1) Removal of collateral such as an automobile from a street or parking lot without the knowledge or objection of the debtor. It is likely that even removal by "jump-starting" a car without using the ignition key will be unobjectionable. It is also probable that removal from the debtor's open premises such as a driveway is unobjectionable.

(2) Removal of collateral with the debtor's consent, or even with the debtor's knowledge in the absence of express objection by the debtor.

(3) Removal of collateral from the premises of a third person in the absence of knowledge or objection by the debtor or the third person.

On the other hand, the following acts are likely to be considered as involving a "breach of the peace" and therefore improper in connection with repossession:

(1) Removal of collateral over the express objection of the debtor, even in the absence of physical violence. The same is probably true where the removal is over the express objection of a third person.

(2) Entry into the debtor's home, garage or other building without consent for the purpose of removal. In other words, where there is a technical "breaking and entering" of premises, removal of the collateral is improper.

(3) Removal of the collateral after threatening or appearing to threaten violence to the debtor or a third person present, whether or not violence takes place.

(4) Removal of collateral by posing as a police-

man or law enforcement officer or by obtaining the aid of a policeman or law enforcement officer who is acting beyond the scope of their official authority.

b. Constitutional Issues

Two constitutional issues may arise in connection with repossession under 1999 § 9-609. The first involves the constitutionality of repossession under a writ of attachment or replevin. The second involves the constitutionality of 1999 § 9-609 as permitting self-help repossession.

Supreme Court decisions have in some instances invalidated state statutes allowing pre-judgment remedies by a creditor against a debtor. In one case, the Supreme Court held unconstitutional several state statutes permitting pre-judgment replevin of property on the ground that the statutory procedures deprived debtors of their property without due process insofar as they deny a right to a prior opportunity to be heard before chattels are taken from their possessors. On the other hand, it has been indicated that replevin or a similar pre-judgment proceeding may be constitutional where the writ is issued by a judge (instead of more perfunctorily by a court clerk) even though there is no hearing prior to the issuance of the writ where the debtor might have a chance to object. However, the Supreme Court has indicated that a state law permitting garnishment through a writ issued by a court clerk without notice or opportunity for an early hearing and without participation by a judicial officer will not be upheld.

In other words, the use of replevin or similar process in some circumstances may be unconstitutional. In determining the constitutionality of replevin following default in a secured transaction, the particular state statute should be examined. The statute might well have been amended in an attempt to meet the constitutional objections.

There was considerable litigation over the constitutionality of the provision of 1972 § 9-503 permitting self-help repossession. Such litigation involves issues that will also be associated with self-help repossession under 1999 § 9-609. The challenges have been based on the requirements under the United States Constitution that there be no deprivation of property without due process of law and on the prohibition of unreasonable seizures. However, the difficulty to challenges in these instances is that these constitutional limitations apply only to *state action*. Such *state action* takes place when there is prejudgment replevin or the like; the writ is issued by a judge or clerk of court and a sheriff or similar official seizes the property. On the other hand, it is difficult to find the existence of *state action* when collateral of a debtor is merely repossessed privately with self-help methods by a secured party.

While the Supreme Court did not consider a direct constitutional challenge to the self-help repossession feature of 1972 § 9-503 and has not (as of the time of this writing) considered a direct constitutional challenge to the self-help repossession feature of 1999 § 9-609, most other federal and state courts that have considered the matter have upheld such self-help repossession on the ground that it does not involve *state action*. Thus, it would seem that the self-help feature of 1999 § 9-609 is constitutionally valid, in the light of a preponderance of decisions to date.

It should be noted that some state constitutions have "due process" provisions that apply even when the state is not involved in the taking of property. Thus, one must also consult the relevant state constitution when analyzing the constitutionality of a repossession.

c. *Steps Permitted in Lieu of Repossession*

1999 § 9-609 not only permits "self-help"

repossession or repossession with the aid of the courts, but also has several provisions which may aid the secured party in instances where repossession is not physically feasible.

If the security agreement so provides, the secured party may require the debtor to assemble the collateral and make it available to the secured party at a place to be designated by the secured party which is reasonably convenient to both parties. 1999 § 9-609(c). This would permit the secured party to utilize judicial help in requiring a debtor in possession of collateral spread out at a number of locations to gather the collateral at one convenient place after default. However, the security agreement must permit this. Presumably, this would be useful in cases where the debtor has collateral such as mobile equipment scattered in a number of places and even in a number of states.

In the case of collateral such as heavy equipment, the physical removal from the debtor's plant and the storage of the equipment pending resale may be exceedingly expensive and, in some cases, impractical. Accordingly, the Code permits the secured party, without removal, to render equipment unusable and to dispose of collateral on the debtor's premises. See 1999 § 9-609(a)(2). Any action in this regard by the secured party must be

"commercially reasonable."   See Comment 6 to
1999 § 9-609.

d. Removal of Fixtures and Accessions

When the secured party has priority over all
owners and encumbrancers of the real estate with
respect to collateral which is a fixture, they may, on
default (subject to the "default" provisions of Article
9), remove their collateral from the real estate. They
must reimburse any encumbrancer or owner of the
real estate who is not the debtor and who has not
otherwise agreed for the cost of repair of any physical injury, but not for any diminution in value of the
real estate caused by the absence of the goods
removed or by any necessity of replacing them. A
person entitled to reimbursement may refuse permission to remove the fixture until the secured party
gives adequate security for the performance of this
obligation. 1999 § 9-604(c), (d).

This provision abandons the "material injury to
the freehold" rule of some pre-Code cases and
permits removal of a fixture by a secured party
having priority, subject only to a duty to reimburse
any real estate claimant other than the debtor for the
physical injury caused by the removal. The real
estate claimant may refuse permission to remove in

the absence of security or indemnity for such physical injury. See Comment 3 to 1999 § 9-604.

Example. Secured Party has a priority interest in a furnace over a mortgagee of the real estate. Upon default by the debtor, Secured Party may remove the furnace, and need only reimburse the mortgagee for any physical injury to the building caused by the removal, but not for the loss of value of the real estate caused by the absence of a furnace.

For discussion of priority with respect to fixtures between a secured party and real estate interests, see Chapter 7, § 7.

A similar provision exists with respect to accessions under 1999 § 9-335(e), (f). When a secured party has an interest in accessions which has priority over the claims of all persons who have interests in the whole, they may, on default (subject to the "default" provisions of Article 9), remove their collateral from the whole. They must reimburse any encumbrancer or owner of the whole who is not the debtor and who has not otherwise agreed for the cost of repair of any physical injury, but not for any diminution in value of the whole caused by the absence of the goods removed or by any necessity for replacing them. A person entitled to reimbursement may refuse permission to remove the accession until the secured party gives adequate security for the performance of this obligation.

For discussion of priority with respect to an accession between a secured party and an interest in the whole of the goods, see Chapter 7, § 8.

§ 7.   Taking the Collateral for the Debt

After the secured party has repossessed the collateral, two possible alternatives exist on behalf of the secured party. One of the alternatives is to sell or dispose of the collateral and apply the sales proceeds to the unpaid debt. The other alternative is for the secured party to propose to retain the collateral in satisfaction of the entire debt, or the secured party may propose to retain the collateral in satisfaction of some portion of the debt. Such retention of collateral for the debt has been referred to as "strict foreclosure." Under the 1999 Code the secured party need not be in possession of the collateral in order to propose strict foreclosure. See Comment 7 to 1999 § 9-620.

In many instances, strict foreclosure is preferable. The parties are often better off without going through the rigmarole of a sale, application of the sales proceeds and either accounting to the debtor for a surplus or (as happens much more frequently) attempting to collect a deficiency from the debtor.

Under the 1999 Code, the secured party may accept the collateral in partial or full satisfaction of the debt in the following circumstances (see 1999 § 9-620):

(1) The debtor must consent to the acceptance of the collateral.   A debtor consents to a partial satisfaction of the debt only if the debtor agrees to the terms of the acceptance in a record authenticated after default. A debtor consents to a full satisfaction of the debt only if the debtor agrees to the terms of acceptance in a record authenticated after default or the secured party sends a notice of proposal to accept the collateral in full satisfaction of the debt and does not receive notice of objection from the debtor within 20 days after the proposal is sent. Such a notice must be sent to other parties in addition to the debtor under some circumstances. See 1999 § 9-621. If objection is received, the secured party must sell the collateral.

(2) The 1999 Code limits use of strict foreclosure in consumer transactions, that is, when the collateral is consumer goods. Where 60 percent of the cash price has been paid in the case of a purchase money security interest or 60 percent of the principal amount of the secured obligation has been paid, the secured party must sell the collateral within 90 days unless the secured party and the debtor

otherwise agree.   Additionally, in a consumer transaction, a secured party may not accept collateral in partial satisfaction of the debt it secures.

(3) Should strict foreclosure occur, the 1999 Code provides that the obligation secured is discharged to the extent consented to by the debtor (full or partial).   1999 § 9-622.   Unless otherwise agreed, the debtor loses their right to any surplus and remains liable for any deficiency only in the case of acceptance of the collateral in partial satisfaction of the debt.   See Comment 2 to 1999 § 9-622.

(4)   A debtor may waive their right to require the secured party to dispose of the collateral.   However, such a waiver is effective only if made by an authenticated agreement after default.   1999 § 9-624(b).

§ 8.   Sale or Other Disposition of Collateral

a.   *Generally; Application of Proceeds*

Under 1999 § 9-610(a), after default, a secured party may sell, lease or otherwise dispose of the collateral in its then condition or following any commercially reasonable preparation or processing. The 1972 Code indicated that any sale of goods was subject to Article 2 of the Code dealing with Sales. There is no equivalent provision within the 1999

Article 9, although it would seem Article 2 would still apply unless pre-empted by some contrary provision in 1999 Article 9.

While in many instances, it is optional on the part of the secured party to sell or otherwise dispose of the collateral, the secured party *must* dispose of the collateral under 1999 § 9-610(a) and cannot use strict foreclosure under the circumstances considered in § 7 of this chapter, above (as where the secured party receives written objection to retaining the collateral in satisfaction or partial satisfaction of the debt or where the collateral is consumer goods and substantial payments of the debt or price have been made).

When the collateral is disposed of under 1999 § 9-610(a), the proceeds are required to be applied in the following order as dictated by 1999 § 9-615(a):

(1) To paying the reasonable expenses of retaking and disposing of the collateral (and to paying reasonable attorneys' fees and legal expenses if provided for in the security agreement and not prohibited by law).

(2) To the satisfaction of the debt owed the secured party. This should include principal, interest or finance charges and any other lawful unpaid charges provided for in the security agreement.

(3) To pay over the remaining proceeds to the extent necessary to satisfy the holder of any junior security interest in the same collateral if the holder of the junior interest has made a written demand and furnished on request reasonable proof of their security interest. Senior interests do not receive distribution as their claims in the collateral are unaffected by the sale.

(4) To a secured party that is a consignor if the secured party receives demand for distribution of proceeds from the consignor.

Note: For an example illustrating the application of proceeds, see the immediately following discussion.

b. *Right to Surplus or Liability for Deficiency*

If the security interest secures an indebtedness, the secured party must account to the debtor for any surplus and, unless otherwise agreed, the debtor is liable for any deficiency. 1999 § 9-615(d). If the owner of the collateral is not the obligor, the owner is entitled to the surplus, if any, but is not liable for any deficiency. See 1999 § 9-102(a)(28). Under the 1999 Code, in a consumer-goods transaction, the secured party must provide the debtor or obligor with an explanation of how the deficiency or surplus was calculated. 1999 § 9-616. For a discussion of rights when the secured party knows that a third person owns the collateral, see Chapter 3, § 5.

Example. Debtor owes SP-1 $10,000 and is in default. SP-1 repossesses and resells the collateral. The sale (properly conducted) brings $15,000. Before the proceeds are distributed, SP-1 receives written notice from SP-2 of a junior security interest of $2,000. The expenses of the sale are $200 and the fee due the attorney for SP-1 is $500. The proceeds of the sale are applied as follows: (1) $200 to expenses and $500 to attorneys' fees, (2) $10,000 to pay the claim of SP-1, (3) $2,000 to pay the claim of SP-2, and (4) the surplus of $2,300 to Debtor. Note that if the sale (properly conducted) had brought only $8,000, the proceeds would have been applied $200 to expenses and $500 to attorneys' fees and $7,300 to apply against the debt due SP-1. That would leave Debtor liable for a $2,700 deficiency to SP-1 and the full $2,000 due SP-2.

In probably the majority of cases, a deficiency will result following the sale of collateral because such sales often do not bring favorable prices even when properly conducted and because some of the proceeds will be applied to expenses, attorneys' fees and like items.

CAVEAT. A number of states by statute outside

the Code have restricted the right of a creditor with a security interest in consumer goods to repossess or sell the collateral and then collect a deficiency judgment. In some instances (particularly when the debt is under a certain amount) the secured party must elect between obtaining a judgment and attempting to collect the full debt, *or* repossessing and reselling the collateral but abandoning any claim to a deficiency judgment. When in conflict with the Code, such statutes override the provision of 1999 § 9-615(d) permitting deficiency judgments.

Where the underlying transaction is a sale of accounts or chattel paper [which is within Article 9 under 1999 § 9-109(a)(3)], the debtor is entitled to any surplus or is liable for any deficiency only if the security agreement so provides. See 1999 §§ 9-615(e) and 9-608(b).

c. Method of Disposition: Public or Private Sale

A secured party after default may sell or otherwise dispose of the collateral under 1999 § 9-610(a). The method of disposition is governed by 1999 §§ 9-610, 9-611 and 9-624(a). This provides that disposition (sale) of the collateral may be by public or private proceedings and may be by one or more contracts. The reference to "public proceeding" is to a sale by auction. The reference to "private proceeding" is to a sale in some other way, such as one through commercial channels (e.g., a sale to a dealer who is in the business of selling goods of that kind).

Although public sales are recognized by the Code, it is hoped that private sales will be encouraged where, as is frequently the case, private sales through commercial channels will result in higher realization on collateral for the benefit of all parties. In this regard, the Code departs from certain pre-Code statutes which required public sales. See Comment 2 to 1999 § 9-610.

The sale or other disposition may be as a unit or in parcels and at any time and place and on any terms, but every aspect of the disposition must be commercially reasonable under 1999 § 9-610(b). The collateral may be disposed of on the debtor's premises if such method of disposition is reasonable. See 1999 § 9-609 and Comment 6.

d. Requirement That Sale Be "Commercially Reasonable"

Every aspect of the sale or other disposition of the collateral "including the method, manner, time, place and other terms, must be commercially reasonable." 1999 § 9-610(b). The term "commercially reasonable" is not defined in the Code, but certain rules are set forth below to assist in determining whether disposition in a particular case is commercially reasonable. These rules are taken from 1999 § 9-627.

(1) The fact that a better price could have been obtained by a sale at a different time or in a different method from that selected by the secured party is not of itself sufficient to establish that the sale was not made in a commercially reasonable manner. In other words, a low price received on the sale is not itself always determinative of lack of commercial reasonableness. However, there are indications from case law that a disposition shown to be at a price substantially under what might well have been received is not commercially reasonable. In particular, if the sale of the collateral is followed by a second sale at a substantially greater price, the first sale may be deemed not to have been commercially reasonable. Also, if the secured party is shown not to have exerted reasonable efforts (as by failure to contact a large number of prospective buyers) the sale may be held not commercially reasonable.

Example. Debtor bought a car from Dealer at a price of $1,395. Dealer assigned Debtor's chattel paper to Finance Company. Upon default, Finance

Company repossessed the car and sold it back to Dealer for $348. Dealer made repairs costing $402 and then resold the car for $1,050. The sale by Finance Company to Dealer was not commercially reasonable.

(2) If the secured party either (a) sells the collateral in the usual manner in any recognized market therefor, or (b) if they sell at a price current in such market at the time of sale, or (c) if they have otherwise sold in conformity with reasonable commercial practices among dealers in the type of property sold, they have sold in a commercially reasonable manner. In this connection, it is recognized that a sale to or through a dealer is a method which in the long run may realize better average returns. See 1999 § 9-627(b)(3).

(3) The principles stated in points (1) and (2) above also apply as may be appropriate to other types of disposition (e.g., leasing of the collateral).

(4) A disposition which has been approved in any judicial proceeding or by any bona fide creditors' committee or representative of creditors shall conclusively be deemed to be commercially reasonable.

(5) None of the methods of disposition set forth above are to be regarded as either required or

exclusive in determining if the disposition is commercially reasonable. See former Comment 2 to 1972 § 9-507. The 1999 Code does not have an equivalent Comment, but it would appear the same rule would continue to apply. See generally, 1999 § 9-627.

Unlike some former statutes, the Code sets forth no period within which disposition of the collateral must be made, except in the case of consumer goods, which under 1999 § 9-620(e), (f) must in certain instances (if the debtor has paid over 60 percent of the price or loan) be sold within 90 days after the secured party has taken possession. The failure to prescribe a statutory period during which disposition must be made is in line with the policy adopted in Article 9 to encourage disposition by private sale through regular commercial channels. It may, for example, be wise not to dispose of goods when the market has collapsed, or to sell a large inventory in parcels over a period of time instead of in bulk. Note, however, that under 1999 § 9-610(b), every aspect of the sale or other disposition of the collateral must be commercially reasonable; this specifically includes method, manner, time, place and terms. Accordingly, a secured party who has held collateral a long time without disposing of it, thus running up large storage charges against the debtor, where no reason existed for not making a prompt sale, might be found not to have acted in a "commercially reasonable" manner. See Comment 3 to 1999 § 9-610. Note further the obligation of good faith required under pre-revision § 1-203 and revised § 1-304.

e. Requirement of Notice of Sale

A secured party that disposes of collateral under 1999 § 9-610 must send to the debtor (and possibly other parties as discussed below) a reasonable authenticated notification of disposition. 1999 § 9-611(b).

1999 § 9-611(c) specifies the persons to whom notice of disposition must be sent. These persons include the debtor [1999 § 9-102(a)(28)], a secondary obligor [1999 § 9-102(a)(71)], any person who has given the foreclosing secured party notice of a claim of interest, and generally, any other secured party that holds a perfected security interest in the collateral to be sold. 1999 § 9-611(c), (e). The notice need not be given the debtor or a secondary obligor if they have waived the requirement by an agreement to that effect entered into and authenticated after default. 1999 § 9-624(a).

In the case of consumer goods, notice need be

given only to the debtor and any secondary obligors. 1999 § 9-611(c)

The notification must be sent within a reasonable time which is a question of fact. 1999 §§ 9-611(b), 9-612(a). The 1999 Code specifies that in a non-consumer transaction a notice of disposition is reasonable if sent after default and 10 days or more before the earliest time of disposition set forth in the notice. 1999 § 9-612(b).

Notice of the impending disposition is not required if the collateral is (a) perishable, or (b) threatens to decline speedily in value, or (c) is of a kind customarily sold on a recognized market. 1999 § 9-611(d).

The required form and content of the notice of disposition is described in detail in 1999 §§ 9-613, 9-614. A "model form" is set out in 1999 § 9-613(5). Although a particular phrasing of the notice is not required [1999 § 9-613(4)] and other information may be included [1999 § 9-613(3)(A)], and minor errors are tolerated [1999 § 9-613(3)(B)], the required contents otherwise include: a description of the debtor and secured party; a description of the collateral subject to the disposition; a statement of the method of intended disposition; a statement that the debtor is entitled to an accounting of the unpaid surplus; and a statement of the time and place of a public sale or the time after which any other disposition is to be made. 1999 § 9-613(1). Additional information is required in a consumer-goods transaction: a description of any liability for a deficiency of the person to which the notice is sent; a telephone number from which the amount that must be paid to the secured party to redeem is available; and a telephone number or mailing address from which additional information concerning the disposition and the obligation secured is available. 1999 § 9-614(1). A "model form" for consumer goods transactions is set out in 1999 § 9-614(3).

f. Rights of Buyer of Collateral

When collateral is disposed of by the secured party after default, the disposition (1) transfers to a purchaser for value all of the debtor's rights in the collateral; (2) discharges the security interest under which the disposition is made; and (3) discharges any subordinate or junior security interest or lien. 1999 § 9-617(a).

Example. D gives a security interest in widgets to SP-1 to secure a loan (D then owning the widgets free and clear). SP-1 files. D then gives a security interest in the widgets to SP-2 to secure another loan. SP-2 also files but has an interest subordinate to SP-1 who filed first. Later, LC gets a judgment against D and levies on the widgets. D then defaults in payment to SP-1, who repossesses the widgets and sells them to P. P gets title to the goods free of the rights of D, SP-1, SP-2 and LC. (Note: If the repossession and sale had been conducted by SP-2 instead of SP-1, P would take the widgets free of the rights of D, SP-2 and LC, but subject to the senior security interest of SP-1).

Under 1999 § 9-617(b), the purchaser takes free of all the above rights and interests (those of the debtor, secured party and junior security interests or liens although senior interests survive) even though the secured party has failed to comply with the default procedure requirements of 1999 §§ 9-601 through 9-628, or the requirements of any judicial proceeding, if the purchaser acts in good faith. See 1999 § 9-617(b).

In other words, the usual result is that the purchaser of the collateral after repossession and sale by the secured party takes good title to the collateral, even if the secured party has not complied with the default procedures (as by failing to give the debtor notice of the sale, selling in a commercially unreasonable manner, or the like), so long as the purchaser is acting in good faith. Note that a sale at an excessively low price might be an indication of lack of good faith.

The 1999 Code also provides that warranties that would run to a purchaser in a voluntary disposition also run to the purchaser in an Article 9 disposition. The secured party may disclaim those warranties. See 1999 § 9-610(d) through (f). The 1999 Code also provides for a procedure by which title is formally transferred of record to the buyer. 1999 § 9-619.

g. *Right of Secured Party to Buy Collateral*

In any instance where the secured party sells the collateral under 1999 § 9-610, they may purchase (buy-in) the collateral. It is flatly provided in 1999 § 9-610(c)(1) that the secured party may buy the collateral at any public sale. On the other hand, the right of the secured party to buy-in the collateral at a private sale is severely restricted; they may do so only if the collateral "is of a kind customarily sold on a recognized market or is the subject of widely distributed standard price quotations." 1999 § 9-610(c)(2).

A secured party also has the right to purchase the collateral at a judicial sale and thereafter hold it free of any other requirements of the Code. This right is unqualified (except by the requirement of good faith) and exists whether the judicial sale is public or private. See 1999 § 9-601(f).

The restriction on the right of the secured party to buy-in the collateral at a private, non-judicial sale recognizes that creditors have been known to over-reach by conducting a sham sale, buying-in the collateral at an excessively low price, and then holding the debtor for a sizeable deficiency. However, that evil is less likely to exist where there is a private sale of goods sold on a market or subject to standard price quotations at the market or quoted price to the secured party. With the requirement of commercial reasonableness in 1999 § 9-610(b), the very limited right of the secured party to buy-in at a private sale is unlikely to produce the abuses that have sometimes existed in the past. The same is true where a commercially reasonable public sale is made or where a sale is conducted under judicial supervision.

In any event, it would seem that the action of a secured party buying-in the collateral will be the subject of close scrutiny if challenged by the debtor. This should be particularly so if the secured party later sells the collateral at a price substantially above what they bought it for at their own sale.

h. Effect of Payment by Guarantor or Like Person

A secondary obligor, such as a surety or guarantor, acquires the rights and becomes obligated to perform the duties of the secured party after the surety or guarantor receives an assignment of the secured obligation, or receives a transfer of the collateral from the secured party, or is subrogated to the rights of the secured party. Such an assignment, transfer or subrogation is not a disposition of collateral under 1999 § 9-610 and does not relieve the secured party of further duties. See 1999 § 9-618.

This provision is intended to preserve the common-law right of subrogation of a surety or guarantor in a secured transaction. If such a surety or guarantor has to pay the debt and acquires the collateral, they become the secured party and the security interest against the original debtor remains. Moreover, such a payment by the surety or guarantor is not a sale or disposition of the collateral following default.

§ 9.   Right of Redemption

Redemption (a term not defined in the Code) means the right to free the collateral from any lien or encumbrance and regain absolute title by payment of the amount due. Under 1999 § 9-623, the debtor, secondary obligor, or any other secured party or lienholder may redeem the collateral by tendering fulfillment of all obligations secured by the collateral, as well as certain expenses, and (if provided in the security agreement and not prohibited by law) reasonable attorneys' fees and legal expenses.

If the agreement contains a clause accelerating the entire balance due on default in one installment, the entire balance would have to be tendered. See Comment 2 to 1999 § 9-623. However, local consumer statutes should be consulted to determine if consumer debtors will be allowed simply to bring current the outstanding debt.

The right of redemption must be exercised before (1) the secured party has disposed of the collateral or entered into a contract for its disposition under 1999 § 9-610, or (2) before the obligation has been discharged under 1999 § 9-622 by the secured party taking the steps to retain the collateral in satisfaction of the debt. See 1999 § 9-623(c). These provisions depart from some real estate law and pre-Code secured transactions law by not setting forth a fixed period of time after foreclosure or sale within which redemption is permitted.

Under 1999 § 9-624(c), the debtor may not waive

their right of redemption in the security agreement or otherwise *before default*.   This recognizes the fundamental rule that no mortgage clause has ever been allowed to clog the equity of redemption.   On the other hand, the debtor may waive their right of redemption *after default* by an agreement to that effect entered into and authenticated after default under the 1999 Code. See 1999 § 9-624(c), which includes an exception in a consumer goods transaction.

It should be noted that where a third person puts up the collateral for the debtor and that fact is known to the secured party, the third person has the right of redemption. See 1999 §§ 9-102(a)(28), 9-623(a).

§ 10. Liability for Noncompliance With "Default" Provisions Under the 1999 Code

The 1999 Code provisions that determine the liability of a secured party for noncompliance with the default provisions of the 1999 Code [§§ 9-601 through 9-624] are set forth in 1999 §§ 9-625 through 9-628.

If the secured party is not proceeding in accordance with the default provisions of the 1999 Code, a court may order or restrain continued enforcement of the security interest as appropriate to ensure compliance. 1999 § 9-625(a). Additionally, the secured party will be liable for damages in the amount of any loss caused by their failure to comply with the 1999 Code default provisions [1999 § 9-625(a)], including loss resulting from the secured party's failure to provide requested information under 1999 § 9-210 [1999 § 9-625(b)]. As to 1999 § 9-210, see discussion in Chapter 3, § 6.

The 1999 Code specifies who may recover damages. It includes the following persons: the debtor; an obligor; and a person who holds a security interest in or other lien on the collateral. 1999 § 9-625(c)(1). If the collateral is consumer goods, a debtor or secondary obligor may recover in any event an amount not less than the credit service charge plus 10 percent of the principal amount of the obligation or the time-price differential plus 10 percent of the cash price. 1999 § 9-625(c)(2).

If recoverable damages eliminate any deficiency, a debtor may recover damages for loss of surplus, but otherwise may not recover damages under previously discussed 1999 § 9-625(b) caused by the secured party's failure to comply with the default provisions of the 1999 Code. 1999 § 9-625(d).

Statutory damages are recoverable in addition to damages recoverable under 1999 § 9-625(b). The debtor, consumer obligor, or a person named as a debtor in a filed record may recover $500 in each case that a person violates various provisions of the 1999 Code including those found in 1999 §§ 9-208, 9-209, 9-509(a), 9-513(a) or (c), 9-616(b)(1), and 9-616(b)(2). Similarly, a debtor or consumer obligor may recover $500 in addition to § 9-625(b) damages for violation of § 9-210.

The 1999 Code devotes 1999 § 9-626 to rules applicable to an action in which deficiency or surplus is an issue. In non-consumer transactions, the secured party need not prove compliance with the default provisions of the 1999 Code unless their compliance is placed in issue, in which case, the secured party does have the burden of proving their compliance. If the secured party fails to prove compliance, their recovery of a deficiency judgment is limited to an amount by which the sum of the secured obligation, expenses and attorneys' fees exceed the greater of the proceeds of collection (including disposition of the collateral) or the amount of proceeds that would have been realized had the secured party complied with the default provisions of the 1999 Code which amount is presumed to be equal to the secured obligation and related expenses unless the secured party proves otherwise. 1999 § 9-626(a)(3). If the commercial reasonableness of the conduct of the secured party is at issue, 1999 § 9-627 applies to provide guidance as to whether the conduct was commercially reasonable.

With regard to the effect of violations of the 1999 Code default provisions on the secured party's ability to obtain a deficiency judgment against a consumer debtor, the 1999 Code expressly leaves the matter to the courts. See 1999 § 9-626(b).

The 1999 Code does provide some secured parties with protection from liability described above in this section of the Nutshell. 1999 § 9-628 is an exculpatory provision designed to protect secured parties from liability that would otherwise result to unknown persons and under circumstances that would not allow a secured party to protect itself. See Comment 2 to 1999 § 9-628 and 1999 § 9-605. Additionally, if a secured party acts under the reasonable belief that the transaction is not a consumer transaction, the transaction will be treated as a non-consumer transaction for most purposes associated with liability of the secured party. However, the basis for the reasonable belief must involve a debtor's or obligor's representation. 1999 § 9-628(c). See also, Comment 2 to 1999 § 9-628.

INDEX

References are to Chapters (Ch.)
and Sections (§)

AFTER-ACQUIRED PROPERTY

AGREEMENT

See also Security Agreement

AGRICULTURAL LIEN

AMENDMENT TO FINANCING STATEMENT

ARTICLE 9

See Uniform Commercial Code (Article 9)

ASSIGNMENT OF SECURITY INTEREST

See also Account Debtor

COLLATERAL

CONDITIONAL SALE

CONFLICT OF LAWS
    See Multistate Transactions

INDEX

References are to Chapters (Ch.) and Sections (§)